A BAR ON
EVERY CORNER

A BAR ON
EVERY CORNER

Sobering Up in a Tempting World

JACK ERDMANN

WITH LARRY KEARNEY

FOREWORD BY ANNE LAMOTT

⬛ HAZELDEN®

Hazelden
Center City, Minnesota 55012-0176

1-800-328-0094
1-651-213-4590 (Fax)
www.hazelden.org

Library of Congress Cataloging-in-Publication Data
Erdmann, Jack.
    A bar on every corner: sobering up in a tempting world / Jack
Erdmann with Larry Kearney. p. cm.
    ISBN 1-56838-737-7 (hardcover)
    1. Erdmann, Jack. 2. Recovering alcoholics—United States—
Biography. 3. Alcoholics—Rehabilitation—United States.
4. Twelve-step programs—United States. I. Kearney, Larry, 1943–
II. Title.

HV5293.E73 A3 2001
362.292'092—dc21
[B]   2001024802

05 04 03 02 01   6 5 4 3 2 1

Cover design by Susan Shapiro
Interior design by Rachel Holscher
Typesetting by Stanton Publication Services, Inc.

For the newly sober,
for the frightened

Contents

Foreword

THERE HAS NOT BEEN a book like this, a book about an alcoholic's long trip to hell and back, told with such grit, empathy, and humor, rendered in such exquisite prose, since *Whiskey's Children,* Jack Erdmann and Larry Kearney's first collaboration. *A Bar on Every Corner* continues where the first book left off, after the madness of active alcoholism—the sickness, the catastrophic shame, the destruction of families—and it traces, with uncommon honesty and humor, the sweetness, poignancy, and slow-motion miracles of recovery.

By sharing his own story—the long downward spiral, the lurches and stumbles toward a full recovery—Jack offers a kind of blueprint for anyone starting out on this path, stories illuminating the Steps that worked for Jack and for millions of alcoholics worldwide.

The soundtrack I heard playing as I read this lyrical book was a merge of old-style jazz, country music in broken-down bars, the clink of ice cubes, grown-ups shouting at one another, the music of rivers and oceans where solace was sought, the cries of children, and the howl of a man who, left to his own devices, could not stop hurting them.

But the miracle is that he learned he was not left to his own devices. He heard *that God could and would if he were sought*. And against the odds, left with nothing much by the end but buttons and hair, he did seek God. And God could and did because He or She was sought. The soundtrack opened up to include the voices of other people trying one day at a time not to take a drink, the sound of meetings in crowded church basements, the sound of his grown children as they met their new father and learned little by little to trust him, love him, want to be around him. The soundtrack includes the terrifying attempts at first sober love, first sober jobs. It includes his beloved jazz, heard with ears finally hearing hope. It rings with the sound of a man who had finally found his way back home.

Someone once said that when most normal people see a cliff, they walk tentatively up to it and peer over, so they can see whether it is a straight and dangerous drop or a gentle gradation down which they might climb to the beach. But alcoholics see the cliff and everything inside them—the grandiosity, the self-destruction, the stupidity, the desperate longing to connect with spirit—conspires to send them racing to the cliff, off of which they jump. Most alcoholics land in cemeteries, mental institutions, jail cells, and Jack has landed in some of those. A very few land with their butts in chairs at a meeting where alcoholics have gathered to help one another stay sober, repair the wreckage of the past, grow into the people they are capable of becoming, and help spread the word of how this is done. And that is where Jack landed, for good.

This book is like landing in one of those chairs. It's one man's song of destruction and redemption, a man with alcoholism's crippling, disfiguring isolation who, by following instructions when all else failed, found himself in a tribe of people like himself. There's an old saying in Texas that God loves you exactly the way you are, but loves you too much to let you stay that way, and indeed, Jack found both parts of this to be true. Accepted exactly as he was, welcomed, encouraged, loved toughly and loved gently, guided, goaded, and cheered for, one day at a time, he left the land where people died alone, sodden and petrified, and came to find a new land where "the flickering light that comes and goes with the sense that we're doing the best we can, for the first time."

These people, his new tribe, taught him that the elevator to serenity and a meaningful life was broken and that he should instead use the Steps. He did. These people walked with him through the Steps, helping him negotiate the land mines of ego and despair, temptation and loss, to a "power [that] doesn't look for more power but relaxes back into love and roams around the room."

So this is a story for anyone who might be needing some help in early sobriety, who secretly believes that he or she is different, sicker or not as sick, who believes that this restoration could somehow happen for Jack, but not for him or her. It is for anyone who knows first-hand the sense of ruin, of corruption, of hopelessness that the new alcoholic inevitably feels. It's for people whose families have been lost to alcoholism and might be found through the sharing of recovery stories. And it is for anyone who just plain loves great writing.

Fourteen years ago, when I was detoxing, sick, scared, shaky, angry, and *nuts,* I called my brother's friend Jack and asked him for help. And he was there, with ears to listen to my pain and the time to tell me this story that you are about to read, of how he came through. His words and humor and friendship will cast light on the path of any newcomer anywhere who is willing to buckle a seat belt in preparation for the wild ride out of hell. It is operating instructions for any alcoholic or relative of an alcoholic who has not given up entirely on the hope of redemption—a super-slo-mo kind of redemption, with kindness, sacrifice, and laughter all beyond imagining.

This book is painfully honest, because telling the truth is the only way any of us gets well. It's also wise, human, and very funny. What Jack Erdmann and Larry Kearney offer here is a lifeline to people at their most vulnerable and helpless, full of confusion and rage and blame in a rainbow of pain, all the very best reasons to drink. This book may be just what they need to get through the day without picking up that first drink, just what they need to make it through another twenty-four hours on the marvelous, changing road to restoration.

I was mesmerized by the first page, astonished by the last.

Anne Lamott
New York Times best-selling author

Preface

I WAS DRUNK for thirty years or so. When I finally got where I was going, to hell, I found nothing there but two voices in my head with their two options—die in fear and misery or just give up and die. So I gave up, ready to die, and got stronger.

There wasn't a thing else I hadn't tried already. I wheedled, pleaded, twisted, demanded, wept, and despaired. The only thing I hadn't done was to look dispassionately at where I was, nod, and give up.

I lost my marriage and my home. I'd called my mother in the night, from isolated phone booths, to tell her I was ready to kill myself.

I scared my kids.

I took my wife into hell with me. I squandered every dime, every piece of energy, every decency, every mercy. I'd pitied myself from one side of the country to another. I wallowed in public places and haunted emergency rooms.

I scared my kids.

I conned psychiatrists, relatives, people who wanted to help, the police, and God, I thought. I lied, cheated, and cheapened everything I ever touched.

And I terrified my kids.

I become an object, a toy reaching for a drink. I sat in a van outside a mortuary weeping, and when a guy came over to the side window and asked me if I was okay, I told him I was crying because my son was dead.

I hope you can hear that. Collapsed in misery, my mind (the other one, the one where the alcohol lived) protected its chance for another drink by killing my son, offhandedly, the way you might swat a fly.

I'd drunk myself into hell, and when I flew through the air to land on my face on the carpet at Duffy's, like a bag on the belt at the airport, it was the only coherent thing I'd done in years.

We seldom recognize turning points. I wouldn't have recognized a truck running over my arm, but when someone picked me off the carpet, I started to give up, I think.

It's not the first solution most of us think of. It's the only solution, though, because it makes a plausible space for God. Nothing else works. No revelation, no sudden clarity, no big hand from the sky—just a first, halting step into real time and sanity.

So this is a book about the steps into life and how they proceed. It's largely about what the newly sober drunk finds most terrifying—time, with nothing to fill it up. How do you live? How do you handle the fear? How do you pass up a drink when your brain is screaming to be made whole again?

This is a record, accurate as it can be, of the drunk's movement toward faith, sobriety, and sanity. It's a scary, tremulous, and painful trip (coming back to life is no joke), in a cloud shot through with an inexplicable light.

A BAR ON
EVERY CORNER

Chapter One

We admitted we were powerless over alcohol—
that our lives had become unmanageable.

It's nice to think that because you come to the First Step help-less, broken, and unwanted that taking it is a recognizably positive thing, encouraging, and making you feel better. But, sadly, by the time you've become broken, helpless, and un-wanted, all you can do is nod your head and say, "Sure, yeah, that's true," even though you don't know, you can't tell. Your head is a shifting, treacherous place, and you can't trust it.

This is the case for the drunk who's gone as far as he can go. Maybe it's not true for the ones who were smarter than I was, gave up earlier, and brought a conscious judgment to the First Step. I felt that wonderful sudden release when hearing the words "God could and would if he were sought," then looking down at the carpet, feeling them, almost crying. I gave up, sat down quietly in an old, threadbare chair, and listened.

1

Unmanageable *is the easier part of the Step. Unmanageable barely covers it: the welter of pain, embarrassment, forgotten packages, unregistered, abandoned cars, and broken walls and windows, unpaid bills, broken promises, and scared kids with breath caught painfully in their chests. Unmanageable is easy.*

Powerless *is something else again. It opens out and seeps and spreads into every corner of everything you ever tried to do, or wanted or cared about. It's the way you feel in the unknown motel room, looking at a broken mirror, and your face in pieces—everything threatening, random, seedy, and hurtful— endless and endless and endless. Your only real relation to it all is through alcohol.*

Oddly enough, when you know you're powerless and say it, you begin to have strength (strength is for endurance; power is for infliction).

But it comes slowly, and the unmanageability fades even more slowly. Thirty days sober I came back to the world like a dead man with nerves, peering into the sunlight off the porch at the treatment house. Had I taken the First Step?

~ ~ ~

I came back to my basement apartment because I didn't have any other place to go. So here I am. The dark is around my head and heart, and I know all I have to do is cross the street to Colonial Liquors.

When I pick up the bag from the counter, it'll be

Chapter One

just the right weight. The drink will blossom in my head, my throat will be warm, and my feet will fit on the ground again. There'll be more in the bottle, anytime I want it. My heart will sing like the music I heard when everything was okay, sort of, and I was six years old and crouched in my father's paneled basement, listening to his friends make music, watching them drink.

I just want to be left alone and not to feel like this. I'm forty-five years old and I have to enter where I live through a basement window. I don't have the key anymore. My nerves are dying and they're all twisted up on the top of my skin. Everything down through the window is dark. People will see me on the ground, wriggling my ass through the window.

My mother did her best. My father was crazy and drunk, but he did his best too. As did my sister, my wife, my kids.

I'm a pretty nice guy. Even when I'm not, I'm a salesman and can fake it. When I'm feeling good and I'm taking care of things, I'm a helluva nice guy. Ask anyone. I don't cry in my beer. I'm just one of the guys.

At Duffy's they told me that when I'm alone, I'm in bad company. Why should I be alone? Nobody wants me to be alone. When I call Mom, she cries because she doesn't want me to be alone. It's not like Dad didn't try. My kids like me. They know who I really am. They'll always know.

The window frame sticks, so I break it with my forearm.

I wouldn't have stopped drinking if I hadn't had to. So I had to, and I know it. I'm powerless; my life is unmanageable. That's what they tell me; that's what I say; and it's true.

(But I'm not going to make it because I cannot go on feeling like this.)

The world is all around me, full of blank faces and liquor stores. What the hell is this? Do junkies come out of treatment and have to walk past giant pictures of elegant women with syringes? Do they advertise opiates on television?

I know that I should go to meetings. I've taken the First Step, but sweet Jesus how can I do this? My life has *never* been manageable. I was an alcoholic from the time I figured out how I didn't want to feel, and that was a long time ago.

"I am powerless over alcohol." You see what the problem is here: alcohol gave me the only power I had, then took it away. The truth is, I don't have anything left to manage. I have seven hundred pounds of fear, a locked door, and a liquor store across the street. Power isn't real. You find that out fast.

Fear is real.

I can smell the apartment through the broken window. I don't want to go in, but I wriggle and twist and

4

slide down the inside wall till my head stops me. At least it's the bed it stops on. My oldest son's bed is against the other wall.

I told them at Duffy's he was dead. I told the other drunks my son was dead. It was a dream. I wasn't asleep though. Steve was laid out in a suit in an empty mortuary room, just me and the shine off his glasses. Then, I left and sat in my ludicrous van in the parking lot and sobbed as if inside my head was only water. And it was all alcohol's dream.

So I start to cry again, feet still on the windowsill, face in the old mattress.

It's a long room like a coffin. When I finally get up, I go to the refrigerator. There's a pint of vodka in the freezer and I stand there looking at it. I'd been screaming and clawing the ground for a drink and the drink had been right there in the freezer.

I look at the bottle. I look at the whole of my life. It felt so good when I first found out that alcohol would make me clean and shiny and *lovable*.

I close the door and walk back down the room at the other end. I put my hands in my pockets. I wish Steve were here. I'd tell him I love him. And he'd know it's true because I'm sober. I think it should work that way. I need to get this stuff out of the way fast, so it won't hurt, and then I can think about not drinking.

Steve isn't dead. I used to hide behind a tree at the

school yard to watch him and it broke my drunk heart that he was all alone. And all that time he was better and stronger than I was.

There are guys who come into treatment to get their wives off their backs. Or they get sent from work. Or the court. But if you walk in like me and you can't handle the stairs, you can't hold on to anything, and you're walking dead, then maybe you've already taken the First Step. That's what I like to think. Please let that be true. Please let me lie down and sleep. Good Christ.

Feeling sorry for myself will get me drunk. Resentment will get me drunk,

Whom can I resent? Anyone. No trouble doing that. I could resent the sky if I tried.

My lady friend Jeannie still loves me. She said so. That's worth something—soft, lying in a warm bed. I'll make the effort here and clean things up. I'll call Mom and let her know I'm all right. Oh . . . Jeannie. Right. I stood her up. We were going to be married and I didn't show.

(We killed our baby too, and I didn't do a goddamn thing about it because, because, it was Jeannie's choice and she had the abortion. Why wouldn't she? The way things were. I love children. I love being with children, but I love fading away in the alcohol better, the rush and the fade and nowhere to find me when they need me. I didn't even try. How could I? What a joke. I'm not doctrinaire; I'm not an across-the-board pro-life tub-thumper—I'm anti-Jack, and I have reason.)

The light is dim but the smell isn't. I can't take the smell. I'll take a shower and I'll go for a walk. I'll fill up my life like it's worth something. Because if I feel sorry for myself, I'll get drunk. I am a worthless piece of shit but I have some great qualities.

I'm sort of unique, you know? My father was a great piano player. He played with Beiderbecke, Pee Wee Russell, and Red Nichols. I have a lot of skills. I have a great sense of humor.

It's dark in the basement room.

I take a shower. There are some clean clothes in the closet. I put them on, comb my hair, and open the door to the light. At the top of the path are the four lanes of traffic. I go to where the traffic light is and lines to walk between.

The Colonial is empty except for Charlie behind the counter. I don't take my eyes off Charlie.

"Hi."

"Jack, Jesus. Good to see you. You look terrific."

No. I look a little better than I did. Thirty days sober today.

"You look ten years younger."

"Uh, yeah. Well I wanted to thank you, Charlie. I mean for putting up with me, the times you gave me food. All that."

"I didn't know what the hell to do. It hurt to look at you, you know?"

"Well, thanks."

"I mean we get bad in here all the time, but you were *bad.*"

Someone comes up behind me. I'm in the way, so I raise a hand to Charlie and turn around too fast, not casual enough, and bump chests with the man. The guy smirks.

"I'll be goddamned, Jack Erdmann. I figured you were dead by now."

I don't even know who he is. Marin County Real Estate for sure. I sidestep him.

"You're a real shock, Jack. Scared the hell out of me."

Pissant. Worthless slick pissant.

"Yeah. Well, that's how it goes."

I am dead. I'm a shaking corpse. I set out on my walk. Things could be worse. Right? Sure. Things could be better too.

The sun was shining as Jack walked down the street thinking about everything that had happened that day and all the bright vistas that had suddenly opened to him. He couldn't wait to tell his mother and give her the check from his first day's work.

I look away from people coming toward me. Who knows what they might know? They might know me. They all have real lives and it's clear I don't. I can feel my steps like they're painted in the sidewalk out in front of me. It's awkward to walk, as if I were at my first high school dance class.

If I were ten years old, I'd be stronger. When I was ten years old, I was scared but I held it together. I dealt with my father. I dealt with everything. In my bedroom at night the moon would come through the attic windows and brighten the white plaster of my foot-high crucifix on the little shiny table, the moon like a spotlight for bad dreams. They gave me the crucifix at school. I was good. I won it.

My father's face could fill up any room he was in. My mother was a substitute world, a soft glade in the tangle. I am a drunk because I am addicted to alcohol, powerless, and because my family is full of drunks all the way back to my father, his father, and the father before that. I am powerless, and horseshit psychology isn't going to help.

God it hurts. I'm an open wound on shoes I don't recognize. Where did I get these shoes?

I pissed on my life like a wino in a railroad yard. I am a wino in a railroad yard. I need alcohol to stay alive.

I stop in the street and think about it. Could I have made it this far without alcohol? This far? Jesus. Could I have made it to, say, 1968? Probably not. I really don't know.

More will be revealed. Take the First Step and more will be revealed.

Jesus, I hope not.

Gerry at the Ross Garage is in the program. He talked to me a long time ago about AA. I'll walk to the Ross Garage and talk to Gerry.

When you can't drink, there's nothing but pure time and space to fall through. Somehow I will fill up my life. Every minute I'm not doing something, I'll be alone. God help me.

Gerry works at the Ross Garage. There's a blue Dodge Colt on the rack and Gerry's staring up at the front suspension.

"I took your advice."

"What? Oh, Jack, hi, how's it going?"

"I took your advice."

He comes out from under the Colt, wiping his hands.

"The program?"

"Yeah."

"I don't believe it. *The* Jack Erdmann. The odds on you weren't good, you know? Hell, you couldn't *get* odds on Erdmann. I'm happy for you, Jack."

He takes my hand.

"How long?"

"Thirty days today. I just got out of Duffy's."

"Ol' Gene scared the shit out of you, huh?"

"No. I don't know. Something happened."

"I know guys who got it all at once."

"I don't think so."

I'm a little embarrassed.

"It was the damnedest thing. I mean, I was just

10

sitting there and I heard Duffy over the PA saying, 'God could and would if he were sought.' I *really* heard that. I felt like I could stay sober."

"Ninety meetings in ninety days. You going to meetings?"

"I just got out this morning."

"You want some coffee?"

"I'd love some."

"I gotta get this car off the rack by one. Why don't you just hang around and drink some coffee."

"Thanks, Gerry." I look at him under the car and try to imagine him as a kid. I've never heard his story. I envy the easy way he is. But he's a drunk too. Like they say at meetings, I want what he has.

"You got a sponsor, Jack?"

"I was around the program once before. You know Tom Kay?"

"Sure. Everybody knows TK."

"He was my sponsor once before."

"Call him up."

"That an order?"

"You know it."

Go to hell, Gerry. I'm ashamed of myself for thinking it. He stops and looks across the room at me.

"You ever going to smile again, Jack? You used to smile a lot when you smelled like the john at the '881.' It's worse now, right? You won't always be like this. Take it on faith."

"It's all I've got."

I hang around for half an hour, picking up tools and looking at them. The torque wrench feels great in my hand.

"I'm gonna head out now, Gerry. Thanks."

He looks at me and drops one arm to his side.

"*It's not always going to be this way!* Can you hear me? You're alive and you're here *today*. You still want a drink tomorrow morning, drink in the morning."

"I hear you, Gerry."

He comes out from under the rack and hugs me with big, dirty arms. What about my goddamned clothes? But I could cry. I have my day planned. I'll walk. I'll do a big circle. Maybe Steve will be home when I get back. It's hard when the street is one long liquor ad. Bars on every corner, restaurants, supermarkets, drug stores, and liquor stores the size of supermarkets with pushcarts for the cases of booze. There's somebody else in my head and he wants a drink, so he's pushing the buttons that always got him one before. I'm just starting to feel him, like you notice a hole in your tooth with the top of your tongue. I have to learn to distinguish between what I want and what I need. They all tell me that.

What I Need

1. Food
2. A place to live

3.   Enough money for 1 and 2
4.   To not be alone

    It's a beautiful day and I walk over Wolfe Grade to San Rafael. The houses off Wolfe Grade are big and hidden. On San Rafael is Lincoln House. Five, ten, twenty times drying out in Lincoln House. I'm a standing joke there. Three blocks up and two to the right is Milani's. A block up from there is Winton's where I'd get my bottles when they let me out of Lincoln House. Two blocks down Fourth is the '881.' A block on the other side is George's. In between is Rafael Joe's where it's dark and cool, with a terrible mural of gondoliers on sickly green water. Safeway is just down the street. A half-pint costs $1.19. At Short Stop you can get a half-pint of Short Stop Vodka for $1.07. To the left on Fourth is United Liquors. Farther down is Ernie's Liquors. Matteuci's, Nave's, the Pines. Much farther out is Speck McAuliffe's and the Coast, Jerry's Farmhouse, the Western, the Two Ball, Smiley's, the Gibson House, the Sand Dollar. I stand on the corner of Fourth and "D" like a run-down windup toy. I step into the street and a punk in a Trans Am takes a tight turn out of the International House of Pancakes parking lot and almost runs me over. My kids aren't like that. They couldn't be like that—I never gave them a damned thing.

    That isn't true. But after I got lost, I lost them. Dave is still up in Tahoe. So is Bridget. Steve is here, I think, with me in the dark apartment. He works at Mountains Are Mountains, a vegetarian restaurant. He washes dishes and goes to school.

I walk. My legs are starting to shake a little. I've got to get very tired. I've got to feel like I've *done* something.

This morning they all said good-bye to me. I stood on the porch at Duffy's and Ali brought her big blue convertible around to the steps. Duffy's has a big, curved drive to the main building. There are five cypresses planted in a tight circle in the middle of the front grounds. Ali sat there waiting for me. She's a fine woman. She helped me through the worst of the horrors. I was very conscious about her body. When I'd watch her walking down the hall in front of me, I'd want to catch up to her, put my hands around her waist, and pull her back into me. But the edge is off the detox now and there's nothing. I'm probably impotent. I'm sure of it.

I sat in the car very still throughout the ride, even when I spoke. She wanted to know how I felt. It wasn't a real question because she knew how I felt, but she wanted me to talk about it, so I did.

"*Believe* me, Jack. You think how you feel right now is how you're going to feel for the rest of your life. It isn't true. *I've been there.* You need to go to meetings and build on the faith you've got. You don't have to go back."

When she let me out on Sir Francis Drake and I

looked at the Viola Apartments, it felt like she'd handed me a bottle of discount vodka frozen in a block of ice and said, "Here's your life back."

I'm powerless and I can't manage anything. Things manage me.

I walk all the way down to San Anselmo. There's loud music from the College of Marin Student Union. Steve goes there, so I go inside and head up the stairs to the balcony. I pick Steve out right away, close to the front. He's got his back to me but I know him. He's in the green quilted jacket with the duct tape over a tear. His backpack's over one shoulder. I head down the stairs to catch him when he leaves. "Steve. Hey, Steve!"

He turns around and peers at me through the crowd. His face owlish with glasses and shoulder-length hair. I slowly walk up to him with my hand out. I'm dignified now. I have the dignity of an invalid. I have to be careful what I say.

"Hi, Dad. How's it going?"

"Really well. Duffy's is a good place." Pause. "I'm through with it, Steve. It's really all over."

"That's good, Dad."

I haven't let go of his hand.

"You were pretty sick."

"Yeah, well, it's all over now."

We drop our hands.

"Everything's going to be fine."

"Great, Dad. Look, I gotta get to work, okay?"

"Sure. I'll see you at the house."

There's a pause in his face like frost.

"Yeah, Dad. Later."

Shit! I did it wrong. Shit! I should have gone over and hugged him. Steve isn't the easiest kid to hug. Why does he have to be such a prick? He knows how I was. Does he think it was fun? Everything's *wrong*. Why can't I start out right? I suddenly think I smell bad again.

I walk.

Things will be fine. I have to keep my balance. I heard a tape at Duffy's that said the drunk in the street always feels bigger or smaller than he really is. The truth again. When I get home, I'll clean up. I'll buy some food on the way home and put it in the refrigerator. I'll call Mom. I'll walk down to Woodlands Market now and buy food and a paper. Then I'll walk home slow, read the paper, open the doors and the windows, clean up, and call home. No, I'll call her first. I have to do that.

So. It's all planned.

At the apartment, I put down the newspaper and bag and open all the windows. In the corner is my mattress. The sour smell makes me dizzy for a second. I sit down away from it, on the edge of Steve's bed.

"Our Father," I say in the murk, "Who art in heaven."

I have taken the First Step. I'm sure of it. The problem is, I'm going to have to keep taking it, every day.

Chapter Two

Came to believe that a Power greater than
ourselves could restore us to sanity.

*I don't know about sanity. I know about relief. I know I need
not to feel the way I've felt; not to be the way I am; not to hurt
like a piece of torn flesh; not to be afraid; and not to have to see
Time in front of me like an empty furnished room, like the
rooms I'd been in with my family that had felt seedy.*

*But sanity? I wouldn't know it if it bit me. When was I
sane? When I felt good? Is that sanity? Are you sane if you feel
good when everything is miserable? Was I sane sitting on a
pony in St. Louis, eight years old? Was I sane hustling real estate? Taking my kids to the movies?*

*I really don't know. I have emotions running around in
me like crazed mice and since this is what I've come to without
alcohol, I have to assume that this is something like the way life
is without alcohol. That's not exactly what I'd look for in a life,
if I had a choice.*

"God could and would if he were sought."

Okay, I did hear that and I knew it was true. (How? The only truth I knew was from pain that had to be knocked out by booze. I had to protect my supply.)

Well, I have to assume that it's true because I felt like it was true, and that's all I've got. There's a physical quality to the truth—it can feel like you've just got your body together again, and the ground is real.

I sought God before, didn't I? When I was ten years old and lying in my attic room with a plaster Jesus gleaming next to me in the moonlight. Did it work then?

I guess not. Maybe. Maybe it just took a while. Maybe it didn't. Maybe I just didn't know, couldn't hear.

Is there a power greater than myself? It would seem so. Can it restore me to sanity? It can do what it wants. Anywhere it takes me that isn't here is fine with me. The problem is it might be God, and I want nothing to do with Him.

~ ~ ~

WHAT DO I DO WITH THE TIME? Who even wants to know me? Why should they? What's the month after this? Say the alphabet backwards. Say twenty-five Hail Marys and touch your nose with one finger. Wade out in your own self-pity and drown in the sump. Time will kill me.

I heard it in Duffy's—right through the haze—"God would and could if he were sought." My relations with

God have never been good, but what I hear is that *something* is capable, if I ask.

Certainly I need help. It's clear to me that the ordinary is insurmountable and the extraordinary is on another plane entirely. I pray raggedly that not too much will be required of me, but I know, because of the life I've led, a great deal will.

Powerless, frenzied, unmanageable, beat to the ground by a chemical. How much trouble should I have acknowledging a power greater than myself when I've already been trashed by a chemical. Was I able to beat alcohol? No. What's able to beat alcohol? A power greater than mine.

I've heard it takes a couple of years for the mind to get clear so you can see how distorted your life had become. I remember my father in his big chair with his arms hanging down between his legs and his fleshy lower lip stuck out wet from his tears and shaking. He was locked in. He wanted me to tell him about the Virgin Mary, and I comforted him by telling him things that neither of us believed. Was there a power greater than my father? No question. Could it have helped? Why not?

I remember my father's rage and his big hands coming at me out of the light. It's not an excuse anymore. He still makes me cry, but it's nothing I can use for justification.

His grandfather was an alcoholic, and he was an alcoholic. I'm an alcoholic. It's a *disease*. Sick families are sick families, and if I pretend I'm alcoholic because my father was unpredictable and brutal, I'll get drunk again.

Came to believe. What an odd turn of phrase. The Steps are strange in their precision. It's not *found proof, decided,* or *suddenly understood,* but *"came to believe"* as if the process were one way, predictable, and final, as if the process of alcoholic dissolution were a movement toward the one place where there's one thing to believe. We *came to it;* it makes sense.

I've got to be able to *feel* it, they tell me. There was the first time I felt calm, hearing the words on Duffy's tape, but that was more *then* than *now.*

I don't pray to a Catholic God, never. Why would I? It would just bring up the Church and that's the last thing I need. I don't pray to any God. I pray to the air. I'm keeping my options open. (For what, huh? Good question.)

I call my mother. "Hi, Mom."

"Where are you, Jack?"

I don't know. Her voice is far away, in her St. Louis apartment with the red brick face where I hid my bottles in the dirty laundry.

"I'm home again."

"Are you all right?"

Chapter Two

There's fear in her voice.

"I'm fine, Mom. I'm going to be all right."

"Are you sure, Jack? I can't do this anymore. You don't know what it does to me."

"I am sure."

"I just can't have any more of those phone calls, Jack. I never know who's on the phone or what they're going to tell me."

"I know, Mom. I was sick, that's all. I'm all right. Everything's going to be fine."

"Well, I wish I could believe that."

Jesus. Please believe it. I can't believe it on my own.

"I'm here with Steve and everything is fine. I know what you've been through and I'm sorry. I can't change it. But things will be different now, really Mom. It's all over."

"Well, I want to see you, Jack. It's not that I don't believe you. You know you were always a wonderful little boy, but I've got to see for myself."

"Sure, Mom, I know that."

"How would it be if I came out for Christmas?"

"It's very small here, Mom."

"I don't need much and I want to see you."

"Well, sure, the kids would love it."

"Are Bridget and Dave there?"

"No, they're with Sarah."

"Well, you tell them Grandma's coming."

"Okay, Mom, I'll do that. They'll love to see you."

"George would be very proud of you. I hope you know that, Jack."

"Yeah, Mom."

I hang up and look at the dimness. In order, I clean the refrigerator, the bathroom, and then the rest of the kitchen. I take the garbage down the hall to the closet. Then I read the paper. I put it down and look around. If I start with my sleeping pad, the worst will be over. I hate to get near it because of the smell, but what if it's still smelling when I have to go to sleep. It's got to be done.

Does God care about this stuff? This stuff is killing me.

I kneel down by the pad and bend my nose to the sleeping bag. It smells like the skin of a poisoned body. I pull it off, bundle it between both hands, and run it down the hall to the laundry room.

I'll sprinkle the pad with baking soda. I pick up a shirt, some underwear, and a heavy pair of socks. The socks clink against the wall. One of the socks has a six-inch bulge in it. It's a bottle, a half-pint, and I stand up and hold it foolishly, tipping it back and forth in slow motion to watch the liquid running.

Please help me.

I take the bottle still inside the sock out to the garbage and bury it in the can. I finish up the cleaning without finding any more. My knees tremble.

Chapter Two

Time is starting to be visible. It's oversized holes between the rungs of a high, thin ladder. I call Tom Kay, my old AA sponsor. He's not home, so I leave a message on his machine. I call up Tahoe to talk to my kids, but there's no answer.

The sun is going down and that's good except for having to live through the twilight.

Please help me.

Why is that? Why is twilight like that? It's just scary.

I put on a coat and walk down toward the Woodlands shopping center. I buy an afternoon paper and sit with it in the Hungry House, drinking too much coffee. I remember the sleeping pad, walk slowly back to the house, and put it in the dryer.

I'm doing everything I can think to do and there's still too much time.

Back on the street. I pick up a couple of mysteries at the bookstore nearer the college. Back in the house, I manage two chapters of some Robert Ludlum book. They don't make any sense.

It's almost dark, though. If I walk slowly, it will take me a while to get to the meeting in the church in Ross. I'll be there early but I can help set up. And I can take a shower. If I'm careful and do it right, I'll get *really* clean and maybe a little relaxed too. The only bad part is pulling on clean socks. They seem tight, and bending over still makes me dizzy. It's a quarter after seven. The meeting is at eight-thirty.

Where would I look?

The church is among the trees on a dark street. Its entryway is bright. There's nobody there I know, not early anyway, so I stand around with coffee. I read the announcements on the bulletin board. I still don't know anyone.

I'm on my third cup of coffee and I'm really shaking. I start to plan where I'll sit because I have to be able to get out fast before the Lord's Prayer at the end. It's too embarrassing to hold hands when you're shaking like this. I don't want the other drunks to think I'm not as together as they are. I eat half the cookies off the counter.

The speaker's a funny guy. I don't laugh, but I can recognize him as a funny guy. When the room laughs, I smile a little and push some air through my nose.

I slip out for the prayer and come back after. I walk away by myself, nice and slow. I'll have to call Tom in the morning.

Steve is home when I get back. It's another big chance.

He's watching the tube.

"It was a good meeting."

"Yeah? Well that's great."

"Could we talk for a few minutes?"

"Yeah, Dad, what about?"

"Well, I've got some amends to make."

"Uh-huh."

24

"I know I was a drag of a father, and I want you to know I'm going to do whatever I can to make it up to you. I love you very much, and I'm going to make everything different."

That's his cue.

"It's okay, Dad. You take care of yourself."

"Well, I need you to know that I love you. I mean, no matter how it was, I always loved you."

"Sure, Dad. I know."

Goddamn.

"It would be a lot easier if I knew how you felt."

Asshole. I'm a hopeless asshole. Why am I doing this?

"I'm really happy for you. I hope it works out."

"Can you still love *me?*"

Stop pushing.

"Sure."

"Jesus, Steve. That's it?"

"What do you want me to say? Sure I love you. You're my father."

"Yeah, well, thanks for the help."

What am I doing? Where's my help?

"This is who I am, Dad. I don't tell people I love them every five minutes. It's just who I am, okay?"

"Fuck it. Never mind."

I wish I could stop. Everything I touch goes bad.

He looks at me from the corner. The light from the TV flattens his eyes in his glasses.

I manage to get to sleep but it's hard. What can I think about that will help me get to sleep?

In the morning I plan out my day. I call Tom Kay and we talk for almost an hour. TK is what they call a "book-thumper." No nonsense, read the goddamn Big Book, and do what you're told.

I read the book. I can't find anything in it that any drunk won't recognize as true. It's all there and I believe it. The only problem is me. I read the stories in the back and there's a piece of me in every one. I read "How It Works" repeatedly.

"God could and would if he were sought."

I'm back alone in the room I had as a ten-year-old with my plaster crucifix. I hate it. I resent it. I resent the Church. I resent God, the Word. I scare myself. I hate God. Sometimes it's like I'm trying to blow up the only thing I've got to hold on to.

Restore me to sanity. "It is to laugh," Daffy Duck says.

Mom gets in three days before Christmas. She doesn't say anything about the crummy apartment. I can see it in her face, but she's kind enough not to say anything. First thing, I drive her to the supermarket and she picks up food for a week. And a quart of Gilbey's vodka and a pint of Martini & Rossi vermouth. Mom drinks now—I had no idea.

"You better pick up an ice-cube tray, Mom. The one in the house is hard to use."

Chapter Two

She drinks every day at five. She has two and the memories start to tumble out of her: George, Pat, what a good boy I was, and what Dad said to her on the way to the hospital. She's sixty-five and discovering the cocktail hour. I try not to get too close to the bottle. I can't take the smell.

"It used to kill me when he hit you, Jack, but he thought he was doing the right thing. And he *always* loved you and I hope you never forget that. We didn't know about the pills in those days. How could I know, Jack? He *did* stop drinking. I just didn't know about the pills."

When you get sober, emotions come flying up from your belly like spring-loaded X-Acto knives.

"Now we're going to Midnight Mass and that's an end to it. I haven't missed a Christmas Eve Midnight Mass in twenty years and I'm not going to start now."

She puts her glass firmly on the table.

"Right you are, Mom. Right you are."

Seek God at Midnight Mass, huh? Not bloody promising.

I have a heightened sense of the ridiculous, but not tied to laughter, just a fleeting, painful, lubricious view of my emotions.

How could I be nostalgic about Christmas? Christmas is a particularly cruel joke. We make our kids think that for one day, everything is going to be all right. They believe it, and if it isn't all right, they blame themselves.

Fuck Christmas.

Maybe I should just die. "I'll just die," I say dully to myself.

Christmas is a bad time for drunks. It isn't ordinary self-pity. It's huge, and it takes in the world. Where's the sanity? Let's talk about the world.

On Christmas Eve, Mom, Steve, and I have a late dinner.

"Jack used to get so angry at me. He was just a little thing then, and he'd get all red and angry when I'd dance. You remember that, Jack? Virginia and I used to laugh and laugh about that."

Steve looks at me quizzically.

"You must have laughed when I wasn't there, Mom."

"Oh, of course we did. You could be so serious; we'd never laugh in front of you." Steve smiles.

We leave about eleven. Our Lady of Mount Carmel is modern. It's circular and set on the side of a hill. Parking is always a problem when they have a big crowd. There's a lot right in front but it's not very big, and the Mill Valley streets are at odd angles, feeding back into each other. The lampposts are hung with Christmas lights. Across the street, at the entrance to the parking lot, Father Tuohy is directing traffic. He's under a street-lamp and his face is very red. As I pull into line, he starts waving his arms angrily at a Chrysler four cars up. I roll down my window in the van.

"Goddamn it!" he screams.

28

Chapter Two

Father Tuohy is smashed. He's hopping around in his cassock like an angry bird. I sit back in my seat comfortably. We creep to the front of the lot. He's waving his arms and sweating. It's a chilly night.

"Goddamn son-of-a-bitch!" he screams at me. "Goddamn jerk!"

I find a space in the lot and smile at Mom.

"Here we are," I say cheerfully.

We have to sit toward the back. As we go in the door, Father Tuohy is chewing out some other son-of-a-bitch. This was worth the trip.

A visiting priest is at the altar and the Mass begins. There's some scuffling going on outside. We get to the Offertory and the door in back to the left flies open and cracks the wall. It's Father Tuohy on the run with a long-handled wicker collection basket in one hand. They've forgotten to take the collection. The priest has raised the Host. Father Tuohy grabs an usher by the arm and sticks the basket's handle in his hand. He pulls it away again, rushes to the aisle, and sticks it under the nose of the woman in the end seat.

"Goddamn jerks," he says. "They think this is a charity."

Mom doesn't look at all.

How about it, Duffy? Is this where to look?

I am looking, because what else have I got? I've got meetings and assurances. I come to believe. This is a process, right? The Steps jump all around and sometimes you're okay with one and another dances out of reach. Take it slow.

Maybe sanity is just quiet observation. That would be nice. Maybe I don't have to react. There is a power greater than myself. That's simple. I can be restored to sanity. I think I can. I think I can, I think I can, I think I can. Fake it till you make it: I've heard that, too, clear as a bell.

Chapter
Three

Made a decision to turn our will and our lives over
to the care of God *as we understood Him.*

*I am still uncertain about "came to believe," and now I have
to make a decision based on it! I don't even know if that's true,
that it's based on the Second Step. The Twelve Steps look like a
logical progression but sometimes, as I said before, they seem to
jump around. One Step may go backward, forward, or leap
three or four Steps ahead.*

*I've made a lot of decisions. I guess I have. I get out of bed
in the morning and don't drink as I'm getting out of bed in the
morning. "I think I can, I think I can," I tell myself as I chug
up the mountain of sobriety with my breakfast.*

*I admitted—I did that. Did I come to believe? I admitted
because I had come to believe. What? That "God could and
would if he were sought." I didn't come to believe that; I
jumped into believing it, leaving God out. It jumped me, really.
Have I missed something? Have I not done the work everyone*

else has to do, and has done—the essential stuff? It would be like me, wouldn't it? Have I weaseled myself into sobriety? What's the prognosis for a precariously sober weasel?

I say okay; I turn my "will and my life over to the care of God" as I understand Him, and what happens? There's a silence in my head. Okay, I'm thinking these thoughts in my head and my head is what got me here.

"Here" is a bad thing (misery, rubble, and fear) and a good thing (the occasional calm, the graceful emptiness). I think perhaps that I need the decision as a reminder that my head is untrustworthy—my head is a crumpled-up sheet of newspaper with bits of pictures and steeply angled bits of headlines.

My head gets out of bed with the rest of me and looks around hopefully for a fearless place to rest while awake. Maybe I'm not reliable enough to make decisions, but maybe the saying I have to tell myself is a sort of control, a sort of regulating tick-tock in the distance. Maybe God (as I really don't understand Him and consciously leave him out) takes the words and sends them back stronger, back and forth, in and out of the Steps.

~ ~ ~

THINGS ARE OUT OF SEQUENCE. I listen in the meetings and hear people going back and forth: old-timers who've been through the Steps suddenly finding themselves back at Step Six or Step Three. I see the Steps in my head as a maze with a gardened, peaceful center.

How I think of God is my own business—as I understand Him.

Of course, I don't understand at all. But I need the still core that comes with the surrender. I need the place where my head stops going around. My emotions are like ornaments on a dried-up Christmas tree. From all their blinking and flashing, I can't sort them out. I make a conscious decision to fake it till I make it. I turn my will and my life over to whatever's there.

There's a woman who talks to me sometimes at meetings in a too-cute, high-pitched voice. I think of Joseph Cotten in the movie *Shadow of a Doubt* (the Merry Widow Murderer), or Robert Walker in *Strangers on a Train* with his hands locked around the matron's throat with a peaceful, glazed look in his eyes.

My mind is going very fast, and since I doubt that my face shows it, I feel like a movie psycho, poised, rubbing his secrets gently between thumb and forefinger.

Schizophrenic is what I am.

I'm faking faith but I have faith because all around me are drunks who made it and they had faith, have faith, and what else have I got? I believe what I'm told and I'm staying sober. But *my mind.* I take it with me on my long walks like a rat in a party hat.

They tell me that when you start to drink like an alcoholic, you arrest your emotions. Got that right. I'm scared, therefore I am. I try not to turn on the television in the afternoon. In my head, I can see every afternoon set in the county—the drawn shades, the blank eyes, and the cans of Campbell's soup still in grocery bags on kitchen tables. It's better to walk.

A dog is what I need.

Steve has friends of his own. This is a surprise. Not really a surprise, more like an insight. I arrested my emotions and as far as I've been concerned, Steve has always been eight years old, standing by himself in the school yard while the other kids play. I'm the drunk watching from behind a tree.

He's moving out to live with his friends. They've been planning the move together. He tells me about it like it's just an ordinary thing in an ordinary world.

I *must* have a dog.

I'm forty-five years old, jobless, living off my mother, terrified of twilight, impotent (probably forever), and yesterday at four o'clock I watched a *Star Trek* rerun.

But it turns out I'm lucky—they've found a place but there's no way in hell they can get the lease. Steve's a student and a dishwasher, and his friends have no credit either. I still have some plastic, so they need me to get the lease. I'll be moving with Steve.

It's a real house in Corte Madera. We'll all have our own rooms. I haven't met the others but what the hell, they'll be kids just like Steve. I'll be a stabilizing influence. There's a yard, and I can have a dog.

On a Tuesday we start to move and I carry out our one big chair and get a sudden, very real sense of the apartment as a living thing with two sticky, vapory paws on my shoulders. Steve has the hood to the engine compartment open, and he's just standing there looking in.

"Hey, Dad?"

"Yeah?"

"Look at this."

I walk around to the back of the van. He points inside to the left of the battery, and I can see the top of a bottle with its green tax stamp.

"Pretty slick, Dad."

"Oh, shit."

"Guess you forgot about that one."

"Throw it out, huh?"

He has to pull to get it out. I must have wedged the fifth of Popov in pretty tight.

"I'll keep it," he says.

"Fine. Just keep it away from me."

"No problem."

I don't want him to keep it. My kid has a fifth of Popov shining in his hand like the light off his glasses. God, don't let this happen. When I suddenly understand that Steve has a life to live, I get cold. I always expect the worst. I don't want him to get hurt, but there's not a thing I can do to protect him. It's a little late.

I go back to the chair at the side of the van and load it in. I strike a pose with my hands in my pockets.

The new house is in a cul-de-sac behind a shopping center. I ask Steve, "What do you think about a dog?"

"Fine with me, but you'll have to talk to Mike and Phil."

What do Mike and Phil have to do with my dog?

"I'll do that."

Mike is a slightly pudgy, blond, clean-cut Marin teenager. He has money in his eyes. "I'm very glad to meet you, Mr. Erdmann," he says. Fine. I can play Mr. Erdmann.

Phil is something else again. He's short, dark, painfully skinny, and his eyes are like that WWII painting *The Thousand Yard Stare.* He's got a city voice, part New York and part LA. We don't like each other. I don't think it bothers him.

At the Salvation Army I pick out a king-size mattress. I look at it and think of having a woman to share it, someone I can feel next to me in the dark, under the covers. Women share beds for a reason. I don't think I'm going to find a woman who just wants to keep warm.

It's a big Salvation Army store and I look down the long aisle at a casual, long-haired woman in jeans. It's not that she doesn't look good to me; it's just that my genitals have been erased. This is what it's like to be a horny old man. I'm sure of it. It's all in the head. You feel like you should be able to do something, but you know you can't.

I'm angry. Jesus, I'm angry.

At whom?

Chapter Three

When I'm outside and back in the van, the woman from the store crosses in front of the van on her way to her car. She has a soft, pretty face and I look away.

The hell with it. I have other things to think about. Like getting through twilight today. And getting my dog.

At the animal pound I pick out a golden retriever. She's only two and of good stock they tell me. She has a beautiful, tawny coat and those dog eyes. I can't explain how I feel. Maybe it's just that I need to prove I can do *something*. Maybe I feel like my mother did, putting me on a pony to be photographed as if the photograph itself, the cowboy outfit and the tired pony, *proved* that things were better than they really were. *I'm a real person,* and here's the dog to prove it.

"What's Phil like?" I ask Steve.

"Well, Phil's a little strange."

"Strange how?"

"Well, we gotta talk about this because I'm pretty sure he's using. He's not trouble or anything like that, but I'm pretty sure he's using."

"Using what?"

"Crank."

"What the hell is crank?"

"Oh, right. I forgot. Methamphetamine, Dad."

"What is that? Speed?"

"Yeah. It's not like a real problem; he just likes it a lot. Mike just does weed."

I look over at him, his shoulder-length hair and his duct-taped jacket.

"It sounds like Phil's a problem."

"He's real cool about it."

"Is Mike gay?"

"Could be."

The world and the twilight are coming in, creeping.

"So you're living with a speed freak and a homosexual who does weed?"

"It's not easy to find roommates, Dad. And *I'm* not living with them; *we're* living with them."

And I'm the farthest gone.

It's a good house, a clean house; it's the seed-place of all the houses I'll live in with substance and dignity. That's how I think about it. I have to move fast to head off the bad imagery.

I turn all this over. I try.

With my big mattress, a dresser, and framed photographs, my room is starting to look like a room. My dog is Louise. I let her come up to my room and sniff around.

I watch her sniffing the huge, empty bed and see myself lying on it at three in the morning with my neck tight and the air full of terror. I wonder how far away from the rest of the house my room will be at night. When I think about night, it floats in my head like a phantom storage locker at the bus station. I'd best go downstairs. I'll cook. Nobody's home but Steve.

"You want something to eat?"

"I gotta leave for work."

"Oh. Yeah."

The living room has a couch and there are curtains on the windows. There's a beige rug. The television is in the corner but it's only four o'clock and I don't want to turn it on. Louise wanders in from the kitchen. What the hell kind of name for a dog is Louise? It's a fine name, and it suits her. I turn on the television anyway.

Phil comes in at five-thirty. He barely looks at me. He's got a heavy suitcase and he takes it up to his room. The door closes firmly. Mike comes in at six-fifteen.

"Hi, Mr. Erdmann."

"Jack."

"Oh, right. Hi, Jack."

"Any calls?"

"I didn't know the phone was on."

"Sure it is. At least the one in my room is."

"You have a separate phone, huh?"

"Yeah. I get a lot of calls."

"I'm gonna cook something. You want something to eat?"

"Nah. I've got some homework; then I've got to go out. Hey, if I get any calls . . ." He picks up the living room phone. "Yeah, this works—I'll leave a little pad here and if you could write down the name?"

"It'll ring in your room, won't it?"

"Oh, yeah, but if you hear it, you know, the door is open."

Phil's friend comes to the door around seven. His name is Matt, he's at least six-three, and he looks like hell. (I should talk.) He's wearing a long tweed overcoat and his hair is a greased-back, shoulder-length helmet.

"Where's Phil?" he says.

I point him the way to the stairs. On the way past the telephone, he picks it up, hears the dial tone, and puts it down again. Louise is blocking the doorway to the stairs. He looks at her and edges by.

"Cool dog," he says.

I feed the dog and make myself a tuna-fish sandwich and a pot of coffee. I drink a lot of coffee. At night it's a problem because too much means I'll be up and down all night pissing. A lot of people have the problem, a lot of sober drunks.

I sit on the couch in front of the tube with my feet on the coffee table and the dog stretched out under them. I just sit there, and the TV moves like a clock. I'm not going to go to a meeting tonight. I just want to stay here and get a feel for the house.

Mike stays in his room. Phil and Matt stay upstairs. Steve stays out. I heard a speaker who said there was a week in his early sobriety he couldn't take one day at a time. He took it an hour at a time and once, for one hour, standing in front of the clock, a minute at a time.

A bottle appears in my head. For the instant when

the image comes up, it's a comfortable thing. That's how I remember it. It's the key to the feeling that you belong somewhere and have something to do. It's like reading *Captain Blood* in the house on Winona Street. No matter what, no matter how it was at the dinner table or how Dad was looking at me, I knew the book was upstairs and that when I picked it up, the pages would be there one after another, solid and real with a drift of cannon smoke.

It isn't my problem anymore, I think; *it's God's problem.* That doesn't really work. I think the drink through in my head to where it really goes, and this time I come out sitting at the end of a motel room bed, punching myself in the face. The smell of the room comes back too, and I shiver reflexively, right from the base of my spine.

Upstairs I can hear Matt and Phil through the wall, a low drone.

I get to sleep all right and dream that I'm going to school in St. Louis. I'm studying piano but the piano they want me to practice on is a huge, cast-iron thing, with levers and knobs and a steamed window. The building is Mary Magdalene High School, and the space inside is huge and broken into secret rooms and hallways.

Not a bad dream, really. It just has the hollow ache to it that my dreams have when they're set in old, familiar buildings and secret, complicated spaces inside. The *bad* dreams are something else again. They're dreams about alcohol, and they come a lot.

The worst dream was the Tahoe party I attended somewhere on the North Shore. Sarah was there, the kids, and my mother. I was standing in the kitchen talking and suddenly I could feel the glass in my hand and knew that I'd forgotten and taken a drink. I'd taken a lot of drinks and I could feel them. I wasn't drunk yet, but I couldn't turn around and un-drink them. I knew it didn't matter that I wasn't drunk yet; it was all over for me.

Bridget came into the kitchen, a little girl, and I said right away, "It's okay, honey, don't worry about it." Everything was real, with no distortion, and when I woke up, I looked at the ceiling in motionless panic. I feared there'd be a bottle next to my bed and that I'd pick it up. I woke up feeling dead, in hell. Even after I knew I'd been dreaming, I felt unreal and dirty somehow.

That's what I mean about somebody else in my head. He's sly—he wants me to wake up thinking I'm drunk already, so nothing matters.

In the kitchen there are still utensils and dishes un-wrapped on the counter. I make some coffee and take care of them methodically.

The sun is shining so I walk around to the shopping center for a *Chronicle*. Louise comes with me. She's very well behaved, just looks around a lot and sometimes

gets stopped by her nose. Somebody trained her pretty
well, I think. Either that or she's just feeling strange.
We walk back, and I say hello to our neighbor on the
right, a middle-aged woman in a blue housecoat, picking up her paper from the lawn.

It's going to be a warm day. I rub Louise's head and
get myself another cup of coffee. I sit down in the living
room and start on the front page. There isn't a sound
anywhere until a wild, swerving screech of brakes
comes through the open door. The open door! I get up
very slowly because my nerves are horrible and I always
think the worst anyway. Through the open door, down
at the end of the street through the trees, there's a
green car sitting at an odd angle. I put the paper down
and go outside. "Oh, Jesus," a man's voice says.

There's a little girl from one of the houses, an older
man with a paper, and the driver. My dog is about
three feet from the right front tire of the green Impala.
Her chest looks crushed and her back is obviously broken. There isn't a lot of blood. She's just lying there
floppily.

"Fucking right in front of me," the driver says. He's
not much more than a kid, and he's very pale.

"At least she's dead," I say.

"Your dog?"

"Yeah."

"Jesus, I'm sorry. It came right out at my turn, you
know? I couldn't get out of the way."

"Yeah," I say, "well she liked to chase cars. I knew it; I just forgot and left the door open."

I don't want him to feel bad, and I can't feel much of anything. I know this isn't good. But I can't feel it yet.

"Just too playful. Not your fault."

A cop car comes rolling out of the Arco station at the corner. He stops and peers, then swings toward us.

"That's a shame," he says. "Good-looking dog. Any complaints here?"

"No."

The guy with the paper has moved on and the little girl's mother is taking her back into the house.

"It's okay, really," I say to the guy as he gets back in his car.

I call my AA sponsor. "Shit, Tom, I got her at the pound. I saved her life," I moaned, "for this?"

"Get off it, Jack. You can milk the guilt all you want, but all it's going to get you is drunk."

"It feels like I killed the first living thing I touched."

"I'm telling you, Jack, get your ass to a meeting and stop playing games with your head."

I turn my will over. My will wants me drunk. This is a conscious decision. Something seems clearer. The one thing the Steps don't say is that you have to take them all the time—whichever is appropriate to the situation.

I go to the noon meeting at the Alano Club. It isn't much; the guy who speaks is one of those "and now I've got a lovely wife and a camper" type. But it's all right.

Chapter Three

The Alano Club is hard core. During the day, it's full of the drunks who can't be anywhere else. We talk, sit, and pick up bits of hope like scavengers on a beach. We're an unlikely collection of people to be holding hands at one in the afternoon in downtown San Rafael: two women around forty, dressed for business; a vet in a bad-looking army jacket and half-laced boots; a teen-age blond with makeup cracking on her face; a biker with slick hair; an old, thin man, stooped and shaking; and a couple of guys in sports jackets, one with un-matched socks that show because his pants aren't quite long enough.

When I leave, I drive carefully and my hands are usually a little too tight on the wheel. I have to turn it all over. Why? Because I have to believe that a power greater than myself can restore me to sanity.

Which power is that? Hell, everything is greater than myself.

My life is unmanageable. Flip-flop. Let God take care of it. I'm just a drunk.

Chapter Four

Made a searching and fearless moral inventory
of ourselves.

*This process stuff is killing me because as I get a little grounded
and start to feel myself as more than an object stamped "Jack
Erdmann," my mind gets more involved, deviously, and it
scares the hell out of me because what goes on in there in pri-
vate is what got me to where I was when I first came to AA—a
broken thing with a lump on its head, screaming inside. Jack
the Lump is who I was. Is that who I still am?*

*All I know is how to be a drunk, and that wasn't sudden,
God knows. (Or maybe it was in the first warm flowering of
the first drink, the sudden "This is a wonderful place and
I don't have to leave it, ever," the high school dance with the
lights, the sudden assurance, the girls talking to me.)*

*I was a deeply religious kid but I turned my back on the
Church because my mind just wouldn't get around the rules
and sins. I could see the Church as it was and cast a pretty cold*

eye on it, especially drunk, when resentment (I'm clear enough now to know) was my dominant emotion.

What the hell is a "moral inventory"? Sounds like confession. Sounds like the Church coming back. I know what they tell me: that resentments are where bodies are buried.

I resent the Church and my father and the world. I resent my mother's inability to protect me from my father. I resent my wife and her expectations. What did she understand about me that gave her the right to expect anything? Do I have moral failings around my father? My father's dead (and was before he died), and anyway, he owes me. Amends to my mother, sure. My children, sure. Sarah, I guess, though she's got some of her own to make, doesn't she?

What if the resentments are justified? Is having a justified resentment a moral failing? What kind of tin saint am I supposed to be? "Bless me Father for I have sinned. I touched myself in the shower, with the soap."

Maybe I even resented my kids sometimes—that they made me feel pain and guilt, that their eyes were a reproach. They stood and watched me as I threw a fireplace log through the plate-glass window. The cold air must have rushed in on them like a bad dream.

I resented the world and its pissy assumptions and responsibilities. How do I feel about it now? Does the world need an apology from me? I think not. I was a moral kid. I was a moral man. I just couldn't act on it because, because . . .

Maybe I'm not "fearless," haven't become fearless. Is that a

*moral failing? What should I do? Wait for a miracle? Maybe
I'm not willing.*

*I know all this stuff is leading toward amends because I
don't read the Steps one at a time and stop at each. Maybe I resent the ones I'll have to make amends to if I sort this out in the
Fourth Step. (The thought comes and goes quickly.) How about
that for a kick in the head?*

*When I sit down and think about it, making a list of my
moral failings would be pointless because they're after the fact.
If I hadn't been drunk, I wouldn't have had them. Is that true?
Was I born self-serving and dishonest?*

*"They are not at fault—they seem to have been born that
way." Is that what this is? Am I just a lying prick and always
will be?*

*"Do it, Jack," that's what I get from the program. What the
hell? I'm willing to become willing to become . . . fearless?*

*"My name is Jack and I'm an alcoholic and the boxes in
the doorway are full of my moral failings. You carry them in."*

"Do it, Jack."

In the dark of my mind am I resenting AA? Oh God, no.
Please help me.

*I have to sit down and write this stuff out. I have to think
about the past in terms of what I actually did. (Are there
people still crying, right now? How many? A woman in New
York who was kind to me, who didn't know any better?) I better sort out my rage. Then what? Then I have to lose the rage
(forgive) and make amends. This is a lot for me. If I watch*

49

very closely, waiting to notice the change when I become willing, that'll take some real time. Maybe I'm just not ready. If I talk about this stuff in meetings, that'll take some time too.

I better not push (they better not push me) because I've always got the rage in there, and boy, can I pretend to get in touch with it. My rages are legendary. I can scare the shit out of anyone, once anyway.

I'll play it by ear. Oh God, please help me.

The Steps are moving around; they seem alive, and I'm not even halfway there.

~ ~ ~

WHEN I GET HOME, Steve is there with his girlfriend, Annie, who is pretty, small, and hippyish. I like her. The two of them are busy setting up for the housewarming party.

"I didn't know," I say stupidly.

I sit down and open the *Marin Independent Journal.* What a miserable newspaper. No real news and lousy comics. There isn't a particle left of the world that I carried around when I was a kid. A draining has happened and the world is flat and boring. I hate the way it feels, hate what it's become, hate what it's made me, hate the blank faces, hate the absence of Captain Blood, hate the guys who never had trouble because they were too goddamn unimaginative to drink, hate the handshakes and the flat eyes, hate the way the light creeps toward twilight. I'm scared and I hate it. I'm scared and I resent everything and everyone who ever asked me to be what I wasn't. Where the hell is Barney Google?

I throw the *Journal* on the floor and head for the shower. Hot water. There isn't anything as good. The spray of water thuds on the back of my neck and when I'm wet all over, streams are running down me. The steam rises up like ghosts and I hum to myself "If I Had You." What a good song.

I stay in for a long time, and the hot water doesn't run out. That's a good sign. I guess it's almost five. I can hear a rustling crackle of music in the living room.

The only party I ever gave when I was a kid was the one in my father's rathskeller (that's what they called the pine-finished basement in my St. Louis neighborhood in the forties). We all got drunk and when my father got home, he threw everybody out. "Goddamn whores," he said. I cringe now in front of the mirror. Still cringe. I remember hugging him drunkenly and saying, "I just want you to love me, Dad." Jesus.

I hate that I had to do that. I hate that he made me do that. Anger ticks in me like a solid old mantelpiece clock, creeping toward a chime.

I talk at meetings. I get out what is inside. I wish I felt a little better when I finish talking. Sometimes I don't feel quite right, feel a little worse, maybe. Sometimes I notice that people aren't exactly involved in what I'm saying. Am I sad or angry? I don't know. Why dig around?

I suppose I could sort it out but it's scary as hell. I can't stay in the shower all the time. "If I Had You"—if I had who? *I could leave the old days behind, leave all my pals; I'd never mind.* If I had who? Pals?

Steve will break down and tell me he loves me in some way that will be real to me. Sure he will; just give him some room. Does he know how hard this is? Does he know how hard it is not to feel sorry for myself? I really need to have my kids get close. What the hell—do they think I wanted to be like that? Mom always loves me, but so what? What does a mother know? She's got no choice. She thought how serious I was when I was a little boy was funny. Ha ha.

I guess no meeting tonight. I guess I'm part of the housewarming (the hell I am). I can watch the kids and be kindly and aloof. I can make them think Steve's got a great old man. I'll come in late and be charming. Is charm worth anything anymore? Is anything I know worth anything? Anymore?

"Hi, I'm Jack the Lump and I'd like to sell you whatever I can. Take my hand and shake it."

I go to my room. I lie there as the light fades and the walls get deep. It's dark when I finally get off my bed. The house is thrumming with a simple bass line. I still haven't told Steve about the dog. It wasn't my damn fault, and if he wants to act like it is, then he's got some growing up to do. Should have had *my* father, Christ; he doesn't know the half.

After a Tiburon meeting (rich little Tiburon, picturesque little Tiburon, like Sausalito where the women made fun of Sarah's clothes), Tom Kay tells me I'd better get started on a Fourth Step. He tells me all he hears from me at meetings is resentment and that if I don't want to drink, I'd better start a Fourth Step.

What does he mean about what I say? I'm being honest. That's what I'm supposed to do.

"I don't know what you mean, Tom."

"I mean there's nothing coming out of you but resentment and everyone can feel it and you're clogging up the room and if you don't stop, you're gonna get drunk again."

"I'm not going to drink."

"You know that better than we do?"

"That's what they all think?"

"Geez Jack, you raise your hand and here we go. The Church fucked you up, your father fucked you up, and when you try to break into a group after the meeting, they ignore you—poor little Jack. You're a walking resentment and you bring people down because you're not moving off the dime, staying right there. We all know what you're gonna say, Jack. You're gonna say it's not your fault."

"Oh."

"Yeah, 'oh.'"

"You think a Fourth Step is what I need to do?"

"It's what everybody else had to do. Are you special?"

(Sure I am. It comes up instantly: *Sure I am.* A motel room comes up with it too, and I'm sitting at the end of the bed looking at myself in the mirror and slapping my own face, hard as I can. Sure I'm special.)

"No."

"It's in the book, Jack. Get yourself some yellow pads."

I don't want to. I don't want to have to hate myself any more than I do. I bounced off my father and he took a swing at me as I went by. I wanted to be saintly and the Church said, "You're damned, you little prick." I go to AA and they look at me like I'm just another drunk. If I'm just another drunk, my father was right, the Church was right, and AA can't fight them.

AA isn't fighting anything; AA is just there.

But the hierarchies, the cliques, the shining stars, the great speakers, and all the clean and neat and loving drunks over there are inadequate and ridiculous (ah, that really hurts). Jack Erdmann over here. What am I doing?

The other Jack in my head is coming back, arguing, wheedling. What does he want? He wants me to drink.

So the yellow pads and the scattered sheets are with me in the dark room. I have the Big Book and the Twelve Traditions, and I've had to sit down with them, tired before I start, scared as hell. Can I hate myself any more than I already do? If I can, will that make me drink again? Who's going to come off the page at me?

After this, there'll be the Fifth Step and TK will want me to share all this stuff. How can I do that? Do I really trust these people? Do I want all my character defects talked and laughed about in churches, gyms, and school basements? Take a Fourth Step to get to a Fifth. I'm going to have to fake this, somewhere along the line.

Tom seems to think all drunks are alike. We're not all alike. And who's going to make a list of the moral failings of the people I had to deal with? People who have harmed *me*?

(I already have a list in my head—a good, solid list, luxurious as a long velvet couch.)

I'm going to drink again, he says.

Oh God, oh God, no. Oh God.

I turn on the light and sit on the bed with my pad on my knees and write. I have a chart for entering my failings at different times of my life. I look at it when I get lost, which is frequently. My life, my outline, is wavering clumsily toward the light. I don't want to see it. Downstairs the thrumming is louder. I put down my ridiculousness and open the door. It's time to go to the living room. Do I have the nerve? Couldn't be worse than my outline, wavering toward me like terror through water, like a terrible fish. There are strangers to look at. They don't know who I am at all. The hell with 'em.

Resentment is what I'm calling all this stuff, but it feels a lot like hatred. Which leaves me nowhere because what I hate most is myself, and I'm really good at it. A nice seesaw—if it is my fault, I hate me; if it isn't my fault, I hate everybody else.

Where's the dog?

Seven or eight people at most. Steve is over in the far corner, crouched on a chair with his clarinet case. He's putting in a reed. The lights are way down and there's a blue cloud of marijuana smoke in the air. I feel like an anthropologist.

(Tom wants me to share this stuff. With whom? The woman who looked at me last week like I wasn't there when I said hello? Lady Bountiful with her dumb bleached hair? I'm a good hater, oh yes—all dressed up with nowhere to go.)

Steve looks up with orange highlights on the flats of his glasses. His mouth is set in a weird way, like it's ready to speak and is amazed at the idea.

(The image of Steve as a little boy—what amazing pain, what absolute grief. I'm hiding behind a tree watching him in the sixth-grade school yard, all alone, off by himself. I wasn't like that. How did he get like that? I made him that way. The Fourth Step leers at me. He would have been like me, I guess, a glad-hand impostor, if I hadn't done what to him? The sad thing is, I'm running from what I did do and denying him his own soul at the same time.)

Chapter Four

My hands are at the ends of my arms, and my feet don't seem quite big enough to handle the sudden balancing act of walking into the room.

The doorbell rings. "Right on!" Phil says. He opens it for a woman in her thirties in a beige raincoat. "Hey, Laura, far out," he says, and as she passes in front of him, I see him half raise a fist to the tall creep, Matt. Matt puts a palm down and slides it forward in the air till it's up like a greeting. I'm still in the kitchen doorway. Phil takes Laura's coat and throws it in the corner.

She's a big, healthy-looking woman, with wide hips and solid legs. Her face is dazed-pretty—she's had a few drinks already.

Sex is dead for me for sure. Can't say that's anyone else's fault, except maybe the Church when they told me I was dirty, a mortal sinner. Maybe they get some of the blame—or maybe not.

I'm standing looking stupid, I'm sure. I feel like I should be turning on the charm. For what? (Is turning on charm a moral failing? Is being charming a crime?)

She pours herself a real drink—vodka in an eight-ounce glass with a couple of ice cubes and a splash of Fresca.

Steve makes a noise with his clarinet. It's high-range grating and he drags it out and down with a lot of vibrato. It makes the glands in my neck hurt. I look at him again but I still can't see his eyes. Annie has gone to a chair in the corner. He starts to play along with the record, out of key, and piercingly loud but working the rhythm very well, floating on top and breaking in his own time.

Phil and Laura slide past me in the doorway. He's got his fingers splayed on her upper thigh. She looks to be about thirty-five.

You rotten little shit, I think.

There's a vein pounding out of Steve's forehead. The record has stopped but he hasn't. It's all his own, I think. This isn't the music I gave him. I get a cold shot of loneliness right through my chest. I didn't give him anything. (That isn't true.) Stop thinking. Stop thinking.

My whole life brought me here. This *is* the Fourth Step. My whole life brought me here and I don't want to be here. My best thinking, my best will, my devious heart.

This is rotten music. This is self-pity. I didn't give him this noise. Steve is nobody I know. Wailing and screeching in upper register, his glasses blank and orange, and a blue vein pounding in his head. When he stops for a second, he reaches to the floor, comes up with a fifth of J&B, and knocks back a huge swallow.

I didn't give him that. *Oh God, help me get through this.*

A girl with short black hair screams a modulated scream and Steve picks it up with a high quaver. Steve is going to hurt himself. He doesn't drink like I did. I could handle it. When I was his age, I could handle it.

Chapter Four

(Fake reasoning goes hand in hand with fear—I'm beginning to notice that.)

Why is he doing this; why is he throwing it in my face? It isn't necessary. Reason and anger slip into grief, grief slips into fear, and fear leaves me perched on this ugly, idiot carpet like an old, old man with a simpering smile.

What an asshole I am. Jack Erdmann's guide to how to drink successfully. Annie comes over with her glass and says she doesn't know what to do. She says that Steve isn't good the way he is, and it's probably the acid, though he's usually mellow behind it.

Helpless anger. Why is she telling me? I barely know this kid. He's different. He has more to do with her. Why doesn't she handle it?

Steve dips into a medium blues and the room eases off. The scene isn't quite as broken. He takes off his glasses with one hand and puts them in his pocket. He peers at Annie down the raised length of the clarinet. He looks at me and trills a low minor.

"I just wanted you to know what's going on in case I need help," Annie says.

"You think we'll need help?"

"I don't know. I've never seen him like this, and these guys are no help."

"Who are they anyway?"

"It's hard to find roommates. Phil's kind of an evil guy."

"Are we going to need a doctor?"

"I don't know. They bring you down on Thorazine, I think. I don't think it's that bad. Just so we both know, we can do something."

Steve is in a little break. He's drinking and talking to the conga drummer. Phil puts on a blues record. *Born Under a Bad Sign.* Give me a break. Steve picks it up three octaves higher and the vein pops out like a snake.

I'm not supposed to be here. This is no kind of place I should be. What about this? Should I be accepting or what? Should I resent? Tom told me don't be a hero, walk away. When it really comes down to it, all I've got is what I've been told.

(Like the Church? Like the Church told me?)

There's the smell now in the room. Enough has been spilled so the air has a flat-sour edge of alcohol. From the smell to the taste is a fast, electrical loop in my head. There's marijuana too, and I wonder what it's doing to me.

I go into Mike's room and call Tom. That's what I'm supposed to do. I feel safer just by doing what I'm supposed to do. He tells me to get the hell out and I say, yeah Tom, I'll do that. He tells me *he* wouldn't try to handle a scene like that, and he's been sober a lot longer than I have.

"If you stay, Jack, you're setting yourself up. You better know that. Get out of the house. Get some coffee. Work on your Fourth Step. Get to a meeting."

Chapter Four

I sit there for a while by the telephone. The clarinet has been a constant for more than an hour. I wonder how they stand it. To me, it's like a wound in the air, slit open by a razor. The vein is so blue and thin in his head. I'm in there for at least an hour, in the dark, my pages are scattered on the bed and all around me.

(Self-pity. I shake myself.)

So I get sober and the world says, "Big deal—here, here's a dead dog for your trouble." It doesn't mean anything—the world really doesn't care what I do.

(Self-pity. I shake myself.)

All the tail ends of fears from the back-there wave in the dark like the spidery streamers in a fun house. My life stopped and then started again, but other lives kept going—the ones I helped make. I've never prayed quite this way before. I don't know what to say. What have I done?

(Self-pity.)

Please help me.

The world is the world. Let it go. *Please help me.* It's odd, but that doesn't feel like self-pity. It feels all right, like maybe I can stay with it for a while.

I get up feeling very much like an old man. There's only the phonograph now, some high-voiced country singer.

Back downstairs ("I have a life, you know. I just had to tend to things upstairs for a bit"), Steve is sprawled on the couch and Annie is sitting on its edge, holding his hand. The vein is still out in his head. It didn't go back when he stopped this time. A drunk is asleep in the chair in the corner. It looks like the party blew out early, probably because of Steve. Mike is cleaning up in the kitchen. Phil and Matt are gone.

"Is there anything I can do?"

"It's all right." She smiles up at me. "Really."

I ask Mike, too, if there's any help he needs. When he says no, I'm dead; I have to go back up the stairs. My legs have a dull heaviness to them. There's a light under Phil's door.

I open mine and I hear them right away. My wall is thumping rhythmically. I turn on the light and sit on the end of my bed. It must be Laura. What is she doing with Phil?

She's thirty-five and works in some office, and when she goes home, she eats something frozen and stands by the oven waiting for it with a drink in her hand. She's very shy, and when she's just drunk enough, she looks in the mirror and likes the way she looks resigned and tough. I know what I need, she probably thinks.

The bed creaks loudly.

This *is* hell. God help me, I feel a stirring in my groin. Talk about moral failings. I go back down the stairs. Annie and Steve are back in his room. The kitchen's quiet. I lie down on the couch.

(No self-pity; I'm just dead tired. It's a good way to be. *Please help me,* you say when you're dead tired.)

Chapter Four

In the morning I hear noises in the kitchen. The sun is just coming through the windows. Laura's in the kitchen in her raincoat, and she turns around as I pad through the door in my socks. She's got about two inches of tequila in a beer glass. Her hair isn't combed yet and her eyes are red. She smiles at me.

"I could make some coffee," I say.

"Oh, that's all right. I'm late, I really have to go." She turns away to drink the tequila, and says, "Hair-of-the-dog and all."

"Take it easy, all right?"

"Oh, sure."

She picks up her leather bag from the counter and holds it against her stomach with folded arms. "Well, thanks for the party."

"It wasn't mine."

"Whoever's."

I get out of the doorway and let her by.

"It doesn't have to be like this," I say, and she looks at me briefly, starts to get irritated, then shrugs.

I read the paper, drink some more coffee, and micro-think about the possible range of future disasters.

I look in on Steve and he seems to be sleeping quietly. He's facing away from me, so I go to the window side of the room and look down at his face. The color is better and the vein has gone down. Annie isn't there.

I go upstairs and get my papers and pen. If Tom says I need to, I need to.

It's odd: when I sit down and start to write again, it seems much easier than I thought it would be. I think about that and feel a flighty edge of a good feeling. Poking around in the good feeling seems to take me back to Laura and the kitchen, her passing me, and my saying "It doesn't have to be like this."

And that's strange, really, because I got nothing back, no response, and I don't know why it should make me feel good enough to go back to my moral failings with a lighter heart. Unless I'm such a self-centered prick, I can take actual pride in things that no one else would think twice about. I mentally shrug. I write for a few minutes, then put the pad and sheaf of papers away.

I'll work on the Fourth Step, as best I can, through the week. I have a certainty about that. I'll finish it, and then I'll see about avoiding the sharing part, the Fifth Step. I hear gossip all the time in AA, and I'm not putting out my life as a ridiculous sad-ass drunk unless I'm sure it's going nowhere. Unless I think it's going nowhere? Good God.

I need to run away. No, I need to go to the pound and get another dog, don't I? Of course. I mean I'm starting over, right?

What a good idea.

And I've got my Fourth Step together.

Chapter Five

Admitted to God, to ourselves, and to another
human being the exact nature of our wrongs.

*The fact is I don't have a Higher Power. I mean I know what
they're talking about and I did use the hill behind Duffy's for a
while. I'm real sympathetic to the whole thing, but I've hated
God for so many years that I don't think I can change. (Don't
think I can change? God.)*

*I have a certain adolescent borderline-sexual acceptance of
the Virgin Mary, but lots of Catholics who hate God and the
Church have that. My mother gave me the Virgin Mary imagery. And I saw her move in the dark church. My little boy's
eyes, looking for miracles.*

*Despite my father's weeping and praying to the Virgin
Mary when he was sick and thought he would die, I never
associated the Virgin with him—my old man, I guess, was
just God.*

And what a God he was—just like in the Bible—all seeing,

powerful, vengeful, unpredictable, brutal, and profoundly vain, eating dinner like a man with a potential grievance, like a balloon ready to pop.

Admitted to God. *Why would I have to? Doesn't he know?*

I told them at a meeting that I hated God and shook my fist at heaven, but nobody seemed to much care. One guy came up afterward and said that if I didn't have a Higher Power, he'd lend me his. Very cute, I thought.

Sometimes, though, there is a sinking peace and a certainty that I'm in the right place and doing the right thing. And where does it come from? Not from me. I've never felt it before, not without a drink.

The question is, what am I going to do? I'm not going to float this stuff into AA and hope it doesn't get talked about. I can hear the voices, three or four at a meeting, drinking coffee, looking at me sideways.

I've written down my life, and a sad thing it is. I've done my job; now I just need to finish out the technical part, the admitting.

Admitting to a God I don't care about. But who else?

Someone who'd understand. There must be two or three thousand guys in the county who'd understand. They're all in AA. But I can't. I can't. So where to go?

Right, I'll go to the Church. I'll go to an alcoholic priest and before I start, I'll tell him it's a confession so he can't tell anyone in the program. I'll have the priest boxed in. Am I slick, or what?

Nah. I have all the moves but they're disconnected some-how, and it's not like it was when I hustled full time and charmed the birds out of the trees with their little checkbooks and stayed apart, secret, and drunk. Something is working in me but it's slow, like snow filling in the ground.

I know about the compassion of the helpless—it's all around me. That's my Higher Power, I think. Where it comes from, I'd rather not know. I might have to give something up. I might have to stop blaming God for what I did—for what my father did too.

I'm hiding and lying while taking a moral inventory. I won't tell God because he doesn't deserve to hear and he knows it all anyway. I won't tell my sponsor because he might be-tray me.

It isn't just paranoia, you understand. It is pure, sad, weak-kneed, vicious, chicken-shit alcoholic being—the drunk in the alley in my head, with the lead pipe, and the thirst.

$$\sim \; \sim \; \sim$$

WHEN I FINISH MY Fourth Step, I sob for fifteen minutes. I can't identify an emotion; it's just sobbing. Life is pointing a shotgun at me.

When I was just a little boy with a BB gun, I shot a mother robin right out of her nest. I didn't mean to. I hadn't thought I could; she was so far away. But bang, and dead she was, with three fledglings still in the nest. I took them home and tried to keep them alive, but I couldn't—just one, for a while, a lovely, brave little thing.

I didn't put that in my Fourth Step (what else?), but it hurts as much as anything else. It's one of the secrets of being human that you learn when you look carefully at your life—feeling it. The seemingly little things hurt just as much as the big things, and for the drunk who's been hiding from feelings for most of his life, any point of entrance has a tidal wave behind it.

I'm capable of accusing God of letting my father abuse me, but I'm not capable of accusing him of letting me kill the robin. That one's all on me.

The contradictions in me go so deep, I have to look behind me all the time to see if I'm being followed by the clown Jack Erdmann, the guy with the fake face and the big feet.

This morning I'm thinking about contacting that priest in the program, what's-his-name, and asking if he'll hear my Fifth Step. Tom will think I'm going to do it with him. So? I know what I have to do.

This morning I'm driving up to Bel Marin Keys to the humane society. The girl at the desk remembers me, so I tell her what happened to Louise and she half-smiles sweetly and says, "How terrible." She has another dog for me. This time it's a collie named Satin. She's cross-eyed and swaybacked with a distinct, endearing overbite.

"I hope you have better luck, Mr. Erdmann."

A reproach?

"I'm sure I will. Thanks."

Satin seems even more docile than Louise, and at the house she gets out of the van and walks up the path behind me without checking out the yard. Steve is awake in the living room, but slumped. I can tell he's still in pain. He looks at Satin.

"Two dogs?" he said.

"Just one. I didn't tell you yesterday. Louise got out the front door and got hit by a car."

"God, Dad, you must feel shitty."

"I'm all right."

"What's her name? She's a good-looking dog." Satin looks at him. "Cross-eyed?"

"Her name's Satin."

"Good name. Tell you what, Satin, how 'bout we take a nice, slow walk in the hills?" He grabs her under the chin and shakes her head. "You like that?"

"Are you all right?"

"No. I need to walk. I gotta get out of the house. I'll go slow."

"Well, go ahead then. I'll put some dinner together. You know what went on last night with Phil and Matt?"

"No. What went on?"

"They were taking turns in his room with that woman they brought."

"He's a tacky guy."

Silence.

"You know I love you, Steve." Shut up, Jack. Just shut up. Why did I bring Phil into this? "You really worried me last night."

"It won't happen again."

"You can do what you want; I just don't want you to hurt yourself."

"Yeah, Dad. We all do our best, don't we? See ya in a while."

I watch them from the window heading up the street. He's not walking all that well. I put all the bottles away under the sink and start some meat sauce for spaghetti. I rinse my hands a lot while I'm working. I find I'll just stand there with my hands under the water. It's soothing. I think about Mom, the house in St. Louis, and the twilight waiting for Dad to come home. I put my hands down in the water and hold them there, fingers laced. Twilight soon, twilight soon.

I hear the front door open and footsteps on the stairs. Phil's back. Rotten little prick.

I watch some afternoon news. The sauce is simmering on the stove and time is going by like a religious parade. Steve must have gone for a long walk. I decide to go to the shopping center and get an afternoon paper. I'm going to be up on current events.

I have a real life too—I've got a new van now (Mom lent me the money); I'm going to school for my real estate license (I won't be sleazy, I won't); and a woman put her arm in mine at a meeting (humiliation to come).

Chapter Five

When I finish the newspaper, I get up and add more liquid to the sauce. I fill up the big pot and put salt in the water. I set out the loaf of sourdough and the butter next to it. The six o'clock news is coming on. I peer out the window, but Steve and Satin are nowhere to be seen. I sit back down. By seven-thirty, I'm scared. Pictures come into my head—Steve unconscious on an empty hill and Satin walking around him in circles; Steve facedown with the snake-vein collapsed and blood coming out of his ears.

I put on a coat and get into the van. My heartbeat is irregular. A right and a left turn take me up to a fire road that runs up the hill and along a little ridge. I have to peer through the window. I stop for shadows. The moon is coming up now and the landscape has a round, compact vacancy to it. The trees are isolate; the only thing grouped together is the underbrush.

I get out in the middle of the road in a dip between two hills and scream his name. It doesn't even sound loud. I do it again, then drive a hundred yards, get out, and scream again. Nothing is moving anywhere. It's like a negative in the moonlight.

I sit behind the wheel with my forehead on it. I make a U-turn and start back down. At the end of the street, the lights are on. I left them on. I stand in the doorway and yell. There's no answer. I drive out again, through the shopping center and across the freeway into Larkspur. My head is going to come off. There's a scream in my chest with a knot in it at the top. I sat crying in a parking lot when Steve was dead, when I'd thought Steve was dead. Tears are coming down my face. If only I knew where he was.

I leave the lot, and as I turn into Tamalpais Boulevard, I say out loud, "I AM NOT GOING TO DRINK." I beat both hands on the steering wheel. The tears are streaming down my face. A horn blows behind me and I look up into the green light. A cop is facing me on the other corner. He puts his turn signal on. I roll across the intersection and his red lights pop out of my mirror. I roll to the curb and breathe. The cop slowly walks up to my window.

"What's wrong with you?"

"I won't drink."

"You want to show me your license and registration?"

I look at him to explain. He sees tears all over my face. "I'm sorry officer. My son's missing, I'm an alcoholic, and I'm trying to keep it together. I had to scream. It's all I could do. You know what I mean? It just came out."

"How long has he been gone?"

"About six hours."

He looks up from my license.

"Six hours? Look, why don't you go home? He's probably there."

"Okay. I'll go home," I say. He doesn't have the vaguest idea what's going on.

"See that you do. And don't drink."

He's smiling at me.

I want to kill him.

At the house, I sit in the biggest chair in the living room. Sometimes I try to read the morning paper, an old John D. McDonald, or the AA Big Book.

As the sun comes up, the gray light outside drains all the warmth out of the orange lamp light. I can feel the panic again. The light creeps down the block and the panic creeps up in my chest. I look at the clock in the kitchen; it's 6:48. There's one cup left in the last pot I made, so I drink it. The coffee is killing me. I head to the bathroom again and as I'm coming out, I hear the front door open.

"Steve?" I yell.

"Yeah, Dad."

Jesus. He's taking his coat off. The back of it is grass-stained.

"Where ya been?" I'm as casual as I can be.

"I just fell asleep. I was up on the hill and laid on my back for a minute, and the next thing I knew the sun was coming up. I guess I was still a little fucked up, you know?"

"Where's Satin?"

"I wish I knew. The reason I laid down is that she took off after a rabbit."

Satin is gone. How long did I have her anyway? Twelve hours? The light is still kind of concrete-tinged and bleak. I don't want my dog to be dead. And I don't want to have to go back to the pound to get her again ("Aren't you having bad luck, Mr. Erdmann?"). But it could be worse. I could feel worse.

Looking at Steve in the raw light, I get dizzy off my guilt and the shininess of his glasses in the dimness.

"We better go look for her," he says.

I just look at him.

"We can drive around the hill on the frontage roads."

"Oh, yeah."

We never get that far because her body's right off the freeway at the foot of a little cliff. It looks as if she fell, then got hit by a car. Steve goes down to pick her up, but I say, "No, Steve, don't do that. I'll call the cops."

"Yeah, okay. I don't want to anyway."

He gets back in the van.

"Sorry, Dad."

"Not your fault."

"Sure it is."

"She was cross-eyed and she chased a rabbit toward the freeway, downhill."

"Yeah. But she was out with me."

"It's not your fault. Leave it alone. Let's have some dinner."

"Two dogs in two days."

"Somebody's trying to tell us something."

"He's picked a lousy way. I don't know what it means."

"Let's get dinner. I'll call the cops."

"Do they pick up dead dogs?"

"I don't know. They'll do something since she's on the freeway."

"Yeah. Sorry, Dad."

He's starting to piss me off a little.

"Not your fault."

We drive off that way, not knowing anything, not knowing how to talk, and doing the best we can.

"I'll go back tomorrow for another one. The girl will be so pleased."

Steve laughs.

"She'll think you're eating them."

"Might as well be."

We both laugh, a little, and I can feel the hole between Steve and everything outside. I put it there, I think. He'd come home every day never knowing what he'd find. He'd get up in the morning and go to a school he hated where he didn't have many friends; then he'd come home to a drunk and an angry mother, drinking too. He was the oldest. It was his fault. I know how that feels, like it's all your fault and you need to be better somehow, to make it all stop. That is just before you decide to hide, and if you never show up, it doesn't matter; it really won't.

Oh my son.

At home I call and then put out the dinner, and we're not too bad together, really, not too bad at all.

Relaxed, sort of. We made it back and we're safe. Spaghetti and bread and we're safe. The vein in his head is back in its valley.

"Go to bed," I say. "I'll clean up."

"Yeah. I'll do that."

After he's gone, I try to watch the television but I can't.

Does this stuff happen to real people? Probably not.

I call Father Malick, the priest over in Mill Valley who's in the program. It's no big deal. I'm smooth, fast, and personable. He says he'd be happy to hear my Fifth Step, and we make a date for Monday. This gives me the weekend to go to meetings and get calm.

I've told Tom I not going to use him for the Fifth Step. He's surprised but "Okay," he says; he understands how I feel, newcomer stuff, edginess about the other people in the program. "Sure," he says.

I'm being reasonable. I mean, what if the stuff gets out into the community to some guy who's going to get drunk next week and stay that way and use it against me? Do I need that? Am I reasonable?

"You know, Tom, I've got to live and work here and if someone . . ."

"Sure Jack, okay."

I can't imagine him not understanding. Of course, what I'm saying to him is that *he'd* tell people about my Fifth Step. How else could it get out in the community. *And* I'm saying that I'm different from everyone else who's ever done a Fifth Step, more important. *And* I'm saying that my life is more dire and interesting and dramatic than anyone else's. *And* I'm compressing the Step to make God and another human being sort of the same. But I just thank TK for being so clear-headed and reasonable.

When I call Tom again, I tell him about Satin, and there's a silence until he says, "Lay off the dogs, Jack."

"I will."

I bring the sheets of my Fourth Step down from upstairs and solemnly arrange them in order and start to read. I have a pen in my hand. There's real emotion up front—St. Louis and Dad and the rickety family—but by the time I'm drinking, it's just a list of bad things, weaknesses, and self-serving lies. Once, I'm calling my mother from a phone booth in Reno, threatening to kill myself, and I feel like the worst person who ever lived.

I cried when I read it last time. I'm not crying now. What did I cry about? It's mostly my children, the way I let them down and did nothing for them, drinking at a distance. Sloth too, some envy, fear, rage—but mostly resentments. I know I'm not supposed to resent, so it's pretty safe stuff for the Fourth Step. Isn't it? I mean, being resentful is a character defect, so why not list the people I resent.

Whom do I resent? Well, I resent my father for brutalizing me, my mother for letting it happen, and my sister for being a goody two-shoes who never got in trouble and never got hit. I resent having to work; I resent anyone who has power over me; I resent having to fake my emotions; I resent *anyone* who makes me feel bad about myself; I resent my ex-wife. For what? Well, her drinking led to more of my drinking and that's what led to the horror and . . .

I wish they hadn't done those things to me, the bastards. Is self-pity a character defect? Something's a little off.

So I go to Father Malick and he's a little surprised that I came to him because we barely know each other, but he's kind, open, and sits me down with my manila folder and offers me some coffee.

"How do you feel, Jack?" he says.

"I'm fine, Father." I look down. "If you wouldn't mind, Father, I think I'd like to make my Fifth Step a formal confession."

He looks at me and pinches his nose between two fingers. He's balding and angular, with gold glasses and mostly gray hair. Fifty-three years old, I'd guess.

"Mmm-hmmm. And why is that?"

"I don't know. I grew up Catholic and it just feels comfortable, like it might be easier."

"You have a sponsor?"

"Sure. TK."

"Hmmm. It's that important to have a priest? I did my Fifth with my sponsor and he was no priest."

I look down again.

"I'm a little scared. I think I could do it easier with the privacy of the confessional."

"Ah," he says, "you don't trust your sponsor."

I have a sudden sinking feeling. This is supposed to be a huge, positive Step and I'm already mired in lies.

"Well maybe I'm not well enough yet, Father. And I know how confession works and I think I'll be okay with it."

"Hmmm. Well I can't turn you down, can I?"

What a start.

"Just for my own information, how do you feel about the Church?"

He peers at me and his glasses are the brightest things in the room.

"Not too good, but I'm comfortable."

"Oh, well, then—comfortable is all the rage."

We look at each other.

"Bless me Father for I have sinned," I say. In truth, I have and haven't sinned in my own head. This isn't going to work. But I have it all down, on paper. Give it a chance, I think; give it a chance.

"And when was your last confession?"

"When I was eighteen, Father."

He sighs.

It takes me three hours. Some of it is easy—the opportunism, the lying, the overriding fear. Some of it is hard—the crippled love, the rejected love, the eyes of my kids, the dead hopes.

I finish and I expect something to happen, but nothing happens. I feel about as good as the time that I improvised a quarterly report.

Father Malick absolves me. I've been here before. "Big deal" is flapping around my head, looking for a place to land.

"Say three Hail Marys and three Our Fathers."

I'm silent.

"You did a good job."

Really?

"I'm sure your sponsor would like to hear it too."

Walking out to the van, I don't feel anything. It's very clear, really. First of all, I don't believe confessing to a priest does much of anything. Second, I don't believe talking to a priest and admitting to God are the same thing. Third, I skipped out on Tom and the program. Fourth, I did it to stay secret.

Why would I want to stay secret? Am I so embarrassed about what I've done? I've heard worse and will hear worse still. What's the point?

Am I keeping a place in my head where I can feel whatever I want to feel because I haven't accepted being like everyone else. Am I special? Will I stamp my feet again, demanding what I want when I want it?

Am I a drunk?

I know just what I did, I know it didn't work, and

the only thing left for me to see is whether there's enough grace floating around to save my ass anyway.

The Steps work back and forth and the farthest may yet redeem the botched closest. And they shimmer and twist when the mind isn't ready. But there's always a place, somewhere, where you can get back in, get back on the horse, forgive yourself. The mind sees them, backs away, sees again, stumbles, gets picked up. And though I have no idea now, it's the Ninth Step that will save my ass and swirl me back to the Fifth.

But right now I'm disconsolate and untrusting and dishonest, and the Sixth Step is in front of me like an elevator shaft.

Chapter
Six

Were entirely ready to have God remove
all these defects of character.

This is worse than an elevator shaft. This Step doesn't have a bottom. "Of course I'm ready, of course I am," I'd like to think. But what about character defects I can't see? The ones I don't know about?

So what? It just says ready to have all of them removed. I don't have to know. Why would I worry about that anyway, if I weren't afraid I might give something up I don't want to? And why would I want to hold on to a character defect, known or unknown?

(Because I like them—because they give me the room that I need to maneuver in. What would I do without half-truths; where would I go without vanity?)

"God would and could if he were sought." I heard that and believed it. It eased my heart and got me here, but now I'm asking a God I have dark thoughts about to take things away

*from me that are me. I mean what else am I? Take away
my adjustments, secrets, weapons, and who am I?—Little
Jackie Erdmann, sitting on a pony in the street with a head full
of fear.*

Were entirely ready. *Is that like willing?* Willing *was
hard enough.*

*(The Fifth Step with the priest? What would I call that?
Willingness? Weaseling? Self-will run riot?)*

*What if I blow it, what then? I go five Steps and then I have
to become something that's all in my head—entirely ready—
and as indefinable as anything that involves the head looking
at the head.*

*That's what kills me—when I'm alone, I'm in bad com-
pany. I've been told that and I believe it. Now the Sixth Step
says "go where you're alone and make a decision about how
ready you are to give up stuff you may not even know you
have." The assumption, I guess, is that I nailed it all in the
Fifth Step.*

*If I just say "yeah" and move on, what does that do to the
other Steps? I already know they're running back and forth. If
I say I'm ready and I'm not, what does that do to the Third
Step? I've heard at meetings that the First Step comes up again
and again, that you have to touch it again and again. If I fake
the Sixth Step, though, it only throws a cloud back to the Third.
How can I fake a Step?*

*I'll get drunk, and the world will fall apart under a paper
moon again.*

Chapter Six

(I already faked a Step, didn't I? Is this stuff good for my self-esteem? I'm supposed to be building it up.)

The Sixth Step is right in the middle and it's lively as hell— it's moving up and down and all around, and it asks me something I can't quite fix my mind on, can't quite say.

I heard at a meeting a story about a guy hanging from a cliff face by a branch and calling on God to help him. God says, "Yes," and the guy says, "Help me," and God says, "Let go," and there's a silence and then the guy says, "Anybody else up there?"

It echoes right here, at the Sixth Step. I'm worried about my mind and what it understands. I'm relying on my mind to get me out of what it got me into. I have a good mind, don't I? It lies to me, steals from me, and cheats me on a regular basis. Now it wants me to put on the brakes because it doesn't quite get it. I don't even know which mind is talking to me. Maybe it's the drunk's mind.

I'll be back here—I know it. Maybe back to Step Five to change how it segues into Step Six. Maybe back to Four. Maybe One.

Maybe I just need to let go. Maybe I won't fall forever. Please help me. *That never hurts.* Please help me.

~ ~ ~

I DON'T WANT TO give up lust. My penis may be dead as a doornail (twinges though—maybe) but I need my lust. I've got only a few things that make me feel alive. I remember the women from the drinking days and the sex on the boss's desk and in the car and the feeling of being powerful, alive, and taking what I wanted with a minimum of fuss, with just my silver-tongue bullshit and a bar tab.

On top of that, I'm not sure what my character defects are.

I pause because I've just done a Fifth Step and I'm telling myself I'm still not sure what my character defects are. I should be sure. What's the problem? The problem is, I'm being pushed toward action, toward giving up everything I need to stay secret and unjudged. Because what could be worse than being judged, out in the open? (Losing my maneuverability and the chance to do what I want when I want to—that's worse.)

Maybe it's easier for me to acknowledge the lust because it has a good Catholic stamp of approval on it. As far as sins go, defects go, lust is right there. Okay, well, I don't mind acknowledging lust, but I'm unwilling to give it up.

I'm not sure about the other stuff, so how can I ask to have it taken away? Do I want my resentments taken away? Where would that leave me? Of course I do. Of course I do. Do I want to lose my ability to lie charmingly? Uh . . .

There are more and more question marks in my head. I ask myself questions compulsively. The Steps require it. My life requires it.

Chapter Six

Rounding all this out is the fact that I think I'm ready, and I want to move on. Jesus, I've been sober, going to meetings, and I genuinely feel myself fitting in the program, wanting to help, reach out. (Remember the one line to Laura in the morning kitchen—the *instinctive* line, the maybe-I'm-not-a-hidden, dishonest son-of-a-bitch line.)

I'm a basket case. Are other guys at the Sixth Step like this? Doesn't look like it. "Fake it till you make it," I hear all the time.

The Fifth and Fourth Steps are compromised, but most of the stuff is there. What's missing?

It's not what's missing, it's what's *there*. Jack Erdmann, con man to the crowned heads of St. Louis University High School, stock broker and real estate salesman, and goddamn good-guy extraordinaire (the flip side of the self-loathing—the bright coin spins two sides in the air and lands heads or tails on the bar).

I've brought pieces of the drunken Jack into the Steps. I've done a Fourth Step, but I'm still not sure what my defects are. They must mean the important defects. I've done a Fifth Step, but not with my sponsor. And my relationship to the defects is under a cloud—I've found one I don't want to give up.

Will I stand up at a meeting and say, "I don't want to give up my lust"? Probably not. Would it be worthwhile? Nah. It would be a red herring and everyone would address the lust problem instead of the real problem—that I'm being evasive, in my head, so I can skate a while longer.

Because what else do I have but my defects? Lots of people have serious defects and they don't drink. God, that's sure true. What am I, a goddamn saint?

That's what the priest in Gibraltar said when I made my confession. He didn't know how hungover I was. He didn't know how much I needed to cover my fear with a gloss of sin. "This could be the confession of a saint, my son." I looked as humble as I could.

Why didn't I read my Fifth Step to TK? Whom was he going to tell? What was there in it that would have been a surprise to any other drunk? What did I save?

I saved my anonymity *inside* AA. I stayed secret. I really think that the others can't see who I am, and I'm scared to death they'll find out. This is insane. It's like the guy the other night at a meeting who said, "The first time I went to a meeting it was on Lincoln Avenue. I had my collar up and my hat pulled down when I got out of the car to walk up the steps. I hadn't had my hat pulled down the night before when I was throwing up on a parked car on Fourth Street. So what was I *really* embarrassed by?"

I think about that. I think about the early meetings with the lump on my head, how I looked, how I was, shaking and pitiful (Jack? nah, couldn't be, not pitiful), trying as hard as I could. So what's different now? I've got a place to live (God bless Steve). I've got an offer to make some money (how bad is that?). I've killed two dogs (please, I didn't).

I'm not useless, unemployable, and pitiful. But I have this other mind, I do, and it's going to kill me because that mind is pitiful. I'm not giving it what it wants, so it's going to kill me. It wants a drink. It wants to be back in a morning with a limited number of options and no moral questions at all when the soul dies and the body says "more of the same."

I'm doing my best. I'm doing my best. But my head . . .

When I wake up in the morning, the sun comes in the window and outside, three blocks to the east, is San Francisco Bay and to the northwest Mount Tamalpais with the greens and the fog veils. It's not a fancy neighborhood but it's quite lovely in the early light, except during the bad times when everything gets dark. Then, Steve is a casualty who'll never come back and that's what *I did* to a sweet, serious little boy who just wanted my predictable love. (My other son, Dave, is better; it's easier to think about him.)

I'm talking to God and I'm hiding. There's this movement from inside to outside in the Steps. I haven't crossed the bridge yet, though I'm being asked to. On the other side is God and there's no way out once you get there, no way to hedge my bets anymore. So, am I ready or not?

The question mark floats in front of my face in a

bright landscape—walking the couple of blocks for a paper, standing over the sink, lying in the dark hoping I'll sleep, and waking up to find everything all right.

Money, money, money. At three in the morning, the idea of money is like a bird with red eyes perched in the dark at the end of the bed. What will I do for money? I'll do what I'm good at. What's that? I'll be a salesman. Oh, really?

Something's not quite right and I find myself trying to look into my soul, but I'm not used to that. I'm only used to worrying, which is looking into my head to find a mirror reflecting my head with a smaller mirror in it, and so on. Where is my soul, anyway?

I left it in Reno in a phone booth. I left it in a motel room in San Anselmo. I left it in my kids' eyes as they watched me throw the log through the plate-glass window. I left it with Jeannie waiting for me to pick her up to get married. I left it with her abortionist. I left it everywhere, like a tip on the way out of a bar.

"God would and could if he were sought."

If this isn't seeking, I don't know what is.

TK is a lovely guy and so straightforward, so clear, that I feel myself at the edges of him like a swamp. He just smiles and tells me what I need to hear, what I should be doing.

Acknowledged we were powerless over alcohol and that our lives had become unmanageable.

Chapter Six

I'm clear there, I think.

Came to believe that a Power greater than ourselves could restore us to sanity.

Well, this is what got me through to begin with, really. I'm okay here, except it's still *a Power greater than ourselves,* which is kind of soft and easy for me compared to *God,* compared to the stuff in my head that *God* brings up—everything from my sad eyes fixed on my ghostly white plaster Jesus in my little attic room in St. Louis to my father, his hugeness, his brutality, his sweetness singing to me, teaching me songs, his bulk in the chair, sobbing, asking me to pray to the Virgin for him. All my endless loops and chains of frustrated religiosity. All the disappointments and bright smiles in the face of all the priests, the sanctimony, and the pain in the world.

Okay, maybe I'm not too strong, right here. And I don't even know about *sanity.* Sanity to me is how my head works day to day. The problem, of course, is that how my head works day to day is what got me where I am. Interrupt my life at any point, any violent humiliation, and what got me there was my mind working the absolute best it could.

Restore my sanity to what point? Before I started drinking? That would be okay, except that then I'd be a kid who's just about to start drinking. Okay, there's something behind my actual mind then that I'll call "sanity." Okay. Behind the receding mirrors in my head is sanity, and a power greater than me can show me where it is. Okay.

Sometimes the light is very bright in the morning. Sometimes I'm walking down the road in the morning light and it feels like I'm whole, just the right size, not too big, not too small, and there's a still place in the center of the world open to me. I try to stay there, but I can't because the world comes in with fear and self-doubt.

Self-doubt.

Were entirely ready to have God remove . . .

This, of course, isn't just the power greater than me, not anymore. I mean, I can wiggle around and keep it that way if I want to, but the word is right there, very clear, and sooner or later I'm going to have to deal with it.

But worse than that is the thought itself—entirely ready. Screw it. If I can't tell whether or not I'm entirely ready, I'll fake it and move on.

How many pieces of fakery does it take before the movement through the Steps grinds to a halt, and I'm alone again?

I sit in the living room chair with the *Chronicle* and a cup of coffee, and I read all this stuff about the world and it's really awful—a terrible place. I have three children I brought into it. What can I give them?

I can give them my sober life, I guess. I can give them something that doesn't change and threaten chaos

every day at twilight. I can give them a proof of my love:
that I'm willing to listen and be humble, take direction,
feel the fear, and walk through it to the other side so
that I can look them in the eye and not feel shaky and
compromised. What's that worth to them? A lot, I
think. Feels like it might be worth a lot.

I'd like to give them money, too, and solid, peaceful
lives. Money, money, money. The paper falls in my lap.

I have no power at all, and it's killing me. I'm sitting
like a lump in a chair with a newspaper and a head full
of self-doubt. I think I need some power and that's
where lust comes in, doesn't it? I mean, there's nothing whatever wrong with sex and it lends a certain feeling of involvement, of power in the world at large, of
being there. If I'm through with sex forever, I don't
think I can handle it. Not right now, anyway. I think
about the woman and her beautiful legs I saw walking
away from me. Where was that?—a store, some kind of
store—and how she made my head flare for an instant.
Sitting in my chair, I can feel the blood moving in my
penis and a twinge again, a little thrill like the sun
coming up.

There's a woman at the Mill Valley meeting who
likes to talk to me, I can tell. She's solid in the program
too, so there's no danger there and maybe if I think
about sex all the time, that will help.

I can't think about anything for too long before the
blood of a wounded dog in the street comes to mind,

much like the sudden panic and humiliations from the rest of my life.

"I need a woman," I say to myself.

(My best thinking got me where I am.)

I am ready to have the defects removed. This isn't lust; it's just the stirrings of new life. And where the hell did I get *lust*, anyway? It's archaic. The goddamn Church won't leave me alone.

(None of what I think is true, but the framework of the Steps is grace made solid and they don't let me fall. They're a catwalk over my worthlessness, so I can look down and say "Oh, right." Do I know this? Maybe a little, around the edges.)

No sex without money. There's a truism, I think.

A guy I know says I can get work selling lots up in Garberville. My history with real estate is dire. I've sold things that shouldn't have been sold. I've drunk more liquor in real estate than I care to think about. Half the people I worked with were drunks. They'd sell anything to anybody. Me too. I'd got to the point where I sold property to get the money to protect my drunkenness. Or you die. No excuse. I should have died rather than live that life. That's how it feels. Hard to go back to a job you think dying would have been preferable to. But I don't have to be sleazy, do I? I can keep my own standards and I sure as hell don't have to drink with them. There must be some guys in the program up there, anyway. They're everywhere, like a secret weave in the cocktail lounge fabric. And I am a goddamn good sales-man. (What that really means is still suspect in my head.)

And not only am I willing to have God remove my defects, I'm going to go to where they were most bla-tant and trust God to take them away.

(I'm back in the attic with my plaster crucifix, trust-ing. I can't stand this oscillation in my head. I need it to stop so I can say, "Here I am, and this is what I'll do." I need to really trust and not look back. But to trust God rankles me.)

The Sixth Step is complicated. "No," TK says, "it's simple. That doesn't mean it's easy."

Garberville. Jesus.

Chapter
Seven

Humbly asked Him to remove our shortcomings.

Haven't I done that? No, you haven't.

Isn't it understood? No, it isn't.

Whom do I talk to? To God.

What was wrong with my voice before, when I talked to God? You were a lying son-of-a-bitch.

When I was just a kid? No, but you were just about to become a lying son-of-a-bitch.

Why didn't he hear me then? He did.

Why didn't he help me? Because.

Shortcomings, sins—what's the difference? Sins are grandiose. For drunks, the word is self-important and grandiose.

I hit my forehead with the heel of my hand.

An egomaniac with an inferiority complex will have a great deal of trouble in approaching God, I think. He'll hear himself praying in his head and think of every sincere lie he ever told. He'll expect, too, that his worthless, weak, vicious, lying self will somehow already be on fairly good terms with God. He'll think he has a special edge.

This is stupid stuff, of course, but when you've just been drunk, when you're only sober a few months and not even sure about that—because alcohol is cunning, baffling, and powerful and you know what you're doing—then you've got a pretty fertile patch of soil in which to grow monsters.

The Seventh Step is all the Steps and then some. I'm not good at praying, though I ask for help all the time. I'm not good at being humble (what a worthless piece of shit I am for not being humble).

I'm good at pretending to be anyone I want to be (mostly on-top-of-it Jack), but if I go to a meeting and pretend to be other than I am, I not only feel like shit—everybody seems to know. Everybody. A salesman at an AA meeting is looking at a very tough crowd.

While all this goes on, I'm sifting through thoughts in my head like a sandbox and I've lost my tin pail with the circus animals on it. At every meeting I hear, "practice these principles in all our affairs." I'm trying to do that even though it's the bloody Twelfth Step and miles from where I am.

I have a life to lead and it won't stop while I sort stuff out. The Steps won't stop either, and sometimes they seem like worms on a plate.

Aren't the Sixth and Seventh Steps the same? No. You may be entirely ready to stop being an asshole, but when it's just in your head nothing happens. Right Jack?

Chapter Seven

*Both these voices share my head and won't shut up. Every-
thing I do, from taking out the garbage to going to sleep, is
commented on. Don't get me wrong, sometimes I feel really
good, but when the feeling fades, my head tends to discount it,
both of them.*

$$\sim \sim \sim$$

THE ABSTRACTIONS CAN GET overpowering, but if I can
prove a bunch of things to myself, then everything will
get easier and I won't be so edgy. If I knew, for example,
that I could work my trade honestly and not get drunk,
that would help. I want to be an honest salesman. I'll
"practice these principles" in all my affairs, and every
night I'll ask God to remove all my shortcomings. I
have to make a living. Steve has his life; where's mine?
I'm the freeloader in a 1930s screwball comedy. Or
maybe it's a crime movie, maybe it's dark and brutal,
and I'm a minor character who gets beaten to death in
the alley. Whatever the movie is, it sure isn't *Captain
Blood* of Jackie Erdmann's dreams.

If I'm not entirely ready, I'll go back, get ready, and do
it again. But for now, I need to find out who I am, who
I'm going to be, who I was when I was unacceptable, and
who the hell is in here with me.

So here's what I'll do: I'll go to Garberville and see
about selling lots. And after I've sold lots and made
some money—and I know I can do that—I'll see about

getting laid. Helena, at the Mill Valley meeting, is just right; she likes me fine and isn't seeing anyone.

Once I know I can sell without drinking and that I can still have sex, it'll be a lot easier to be humble.

(What?)

Well, I need positive reinforcement. And if I can still perform sexually, I'll be able to ask God to remove my lust. It'll make more sense that way.

(I've heard it said that it's a bad thing to think you know more about yourself than God does.)

I can get in my VW van and head up to Garberville and Shelter Cove, an oceanfront property built into the face of a curve in the Coast Range. Down at the center of the development there are two streets of actual houses and these, I'm told, are hooked up to sewers. The rest of the project consists of lots and most don't have sewer hookups and never will—the land is too steep.

The manager is Eddie Falco, crooked as they come. He gives informational dinner parties, then has potential buyers flown in on DC-10s to see the place. His hustler agents descend on them like locusts. There's a restaurant and clubhouse on site and trailers for salesmen to live in. Most of them drink like fish.

When I get there, I have a feeling of hopelessness that seeps all the way to my shoes. This is the past in stinking grave clothes. *I don't have to do anything I don't want to,* I think, and *Please God, remove these shortcomings.*

I'm looking around and a couple gets out of a Mercedes in the downtown area. I saunter over and start to talk the easy bullshit talk. They're looking for a vacation place and pretty much want what we've got, so it's not a hard sell. I take them to a lot I've never seen before and play gracious, charming, affable, forthright, honest, easygoing, not desperate at all, but concerned with their needs, their children, their resources, quick to smile though serious and competent, comfortable Jack, ingratiating Jack, sign-right-here Jack. And that's what I get them to do, by God, and right out of my van I walk them up to the office and show them off to Eddie, who looks at me as if I'm from heaven and jumps up to pull up the chairs. "Hi, I'm Eddie Falco. Terrific day huh? Beautiful day."

Jack's back.

I go to the club with Eddie and meet the others. "This is a goddamn salesman and I want you to watch him like a goddamn hawk and learn something. A goddamn salesman, like I told you about, you know? Cold off the road, he brings me a closed deal. So pay attention. Learn something."

Down the bar is a guy nursing a mineral water, so I wander over and ask him if he's a friend of Bill Wilson's and he says "Yeah," turning around, putting out his hand. His name is Tom O'Brien and he's a gentleman, a nice guy, and I feel like maybe I'll live. Hell, I already have money, and now I have support.

Now about the sex.

Anyone who's lived his entire adult life drunk can tell you that the first sober sex is terrifying. You have no idea. You don't know how it will be, or how you will be, or who you'll be, for that matter.

Helena is a sweet woman, blondish, long-legged, with full lips and a great laugh. She's been sober about a year and a half. I'm Jack Erdmann, I've been sober for eight months, and my new part-time home is a trailer. It's a pretty good trailer, clean and new, but trailer it still is, temporary, and a little embarrassing.

Garberville is about five hours up the coast. The trailer's on the site, about forty minutes from town, right on the ocean in a cove with an airstrip that will take DC-10s. Two rows of downtown houses and the coastal mountain foothills rise up soft green, rocky, and treed, steep.

They've been selling the steep lots in Europe, even though they know they'll need septic tanks and the ground is too steep to take them. And I know that. So I'm going into a place I shouldn't be, for money.

I don't have to be dishonest or do anything dishonest. I just have to sell the lots I know are buildable and on a sewer line. I've already sold the first. I just have to keep selling and cast a cold eye on the others with their bullshit alcohol bonhomie.

(It's kind of attractive though, and I find myself

insanely nostalgic as I watch them lurching hungover from their trailers every morning. They have limited things to do—sell a lot, get drunk. The nostalgia says it's a pretty good life. My God.)

While standing back and watching the thievery and the drinking, I can find out if my lust still works, that too. What a deal! It has dead drunk in a ditch written all over it.

It's not like I haven't used women before.

The one who always comes to mind is Barbara, in New York, in the Village, sweet, drunk, caring, and lost. She took care of me when I was sick and crazed, and then when I was well, I just walked away. What else could I do? I was married with kids. (That doesn't work at all, because I was making the lives of my wife and kids hell.)

This, I guess, is not so bad, because Helana and I are both in the same place, fighting the same demons. We are pretty nice to each other, we're not lying, and I don't have any expectations and neither, I like to think, does she. We just want to get laid and have some fun.

Maybe, of course, it won't work and I'll be stuck here all weekend with a horde of crazed drunks and a woman sitting in the trailer thinking about getting home and away from my sad impotence. That won't happen; no, that wouldn't be good at all.

I'm fond of Helena, I like being with her, and I find

her attractive, but no matter how I slip and sidle around, trying to see from a different angle, I'm still (1) using her and (2) scared to death.

I haven't even considered the possibility that she might be doing the same thing—trying it out—but then self-centeredness isn't unknown to me. (Did I put that in my Fourth Step?)

So up we go. Helena has a big picnic basket with her, but then I get involved talking to another new guy and Helena says she'll go back to the trailer. Something like a wedding night is how it feels, and I have old movie images in my head of flounced nightgowns and bride-groom stumbling. But when I get back (the night is beautiful facing the hills, the stars out, and trees in a pale moon), Helena is perched on the edge of the couch eating fried chicken in huge, torn mouthfuls. She smiles.

"I guess I didn't mention I'm bulimic," she says, and tries to giggle. "I've got the drinking stopped but I can't do everything at once, you know?"

I shrug. "I wouldn't expect it. You're not going to eat all night, huh?"

She laughs again, but there's a real edge of worry and frailty in it. "Just let me have the wing, one more wing."

I take a shower and hear her through the water going out back on the little porch and throwing up into the grass. Well, I think, she must pray about it and ask for it to be removed, though I don't know exactly what kind of serious defect it is to overeat and throw up. Not much of one. Not much of a pain to others. I hope she brushes her teeth, I think, then get a little shudder of remorse. For what? I was just being funny in my head.

"I humbly ask you to remove these shortcomings," I say in the steam. This "you" stuff makes me edgy. It makes me feel like a jerk, but I don't know what else to say.

In the narrow bed, it's like I have no center. I'm just clumsy extremities and the ludicrousness of what I'm doing is all over my mind, which is all over everything. *Do what? You can't be serious.*

There really is no problem—everything works fine— it's just that it takes three or four days for us to actually fit our bodies together. But it all goes pretty well and afterward I can lie there with her sleeping head in the curve of my arm and look out the little side-window at the stars and think, "Do I deserve this? Probably not."

The weekend is okay and there don't seem to be any expectations kicking around, and except for the occasional sound of Helena throwing up off the porch, everything is almost low-key, television normal. We drive back comfortably. I have a good line on a sale and Helena's affectionate. We stop in Garberville and she refills her picnic basket.

I'm feeling pretty good. Later, I learn that my daughter, Bridget, is coming to live with us and it makes me terribly happy because Bridget is the light of my life. She's going to be going to San Francisco State and will need a place to stay, so what's the problem? We'll ask the roommates to move and we'll all have our rooms and our separate lives but together again. Bridget is my darling.

She does come to live with us. The sun comes up every morning and sets every night. I'm in a meeting and I'm thinking about the Seventh Step all the time, evaluating my humility.

Helena and I see each other in an offhand way and it's nice—we really have no expectations—and after a while she moves on and no harm done, I guess.

Dave is full of plans, music, club dates, and girlfriends. Dave is kind of a miracle—he seems not to have taken much with him from the old days. He's easy and relaxed. Bridget is Bridget, I think—sunny and bright and responsible. Steve is another matter, and we recognize each other every morning, every time we pass in the hall. There's always the little, barely noticeable shock of recognition. Sometimes we can look each other in the eyes and sometimes we can't. Sometimes we're embarrassed to be who we are and to have lived through the things we have. Sometimes I wish he weren't there to remind me. I never let the thought get far, but I can feel it kicking around. Steve is a tormented guy, and I know where he got it.

There's nothing I can do. What can I do?

I'm not thinking much about Dave and Bridget. It's more comfortable to imagine that they came through pretty clean. Maybe they just have better defenses.

What the hell? What the hell can I do?

Well, I'm making money and I still have one credit card that works so I think to myself, *It's the summer coming up and I could use the card to buy Steve and Bridget tickets to Europe. I could do that. They'd love it. They'd love me for it. I can start making amends now. Dave is deep in other things and I don't have to worry that he'll feel left out.*

So that's what I do. I sit Steve and Bridget down in the living room and tell them I want to send them to Europe and they're deeply surprised, I can see. However, I don't see the sparkles of "Dad always loved us; Dad was always great," that I'd like to see. Still, I understand fairly well that I'm in a process—we all are—and that I can't expect everything at once, especially not from Steve with his difficult eyes and the pain he wears like a shirt. (He *could* lighten up a little; he *could*.)

But everything is okay; everything is moving. At night, I look back on the day and try to figure what I've done wrong. There isn't a hell of a lot.

When I look at my shortcomings, they're easier to see than they were after my Fifth Step. That's a good thing. Resentment, self-pity, chronic fear, sloth, avoidance, self-will run riot—fill in the blanks—but I find when I identify them more carefully, look at them individually instead of in a blanket of anxiety and self-loathing, they're more manageable.

The meetings accrue like grace in the bank, like sanity on the installment plan. The rooms are full of their own odd light and when a meeting is right, when everything is working, there's a relaxed radiance, like the imagined church we all wanted to go to.

"I'm doing all right," I think.

Well, I should give the kids some cash too, because maybe something will come up, something special, and they won't have the money. So I tell Steve I'm giving him five hundred dollars and all hell breaks loose.

It's afternoon and the living room is very bright. Steve is lying on the couch reading. He's taller than I am and thinner, wiry. He's got on an old army jacket, though it's not cold.

"Here," I say, handing him the money. He doesn't put the book down, just looks at it and says, "It's okay, Dad; we don't need it."

"No, really. I want you to take it. If nothing else, you can have yourselves a really good dinner."

"It's okay. Keep it."

"What's the problem?"

"No problem." He lets his left arm fall to the floor, holding the book. "I just don't want the money."

"Well how about Bridget?"

"Let it go, Dad."

"I don't want to let it go. I just want you to have it in case."

"In case what?" His head is just barely turned to me. He's taking off his glasses.

"I don't know. Emergencies? Special occasions?"

"I want to go with the money I earn for the trip. I want to go with my own money in my pocket. I'm looking forward to putting together the money."

I look at him, then toward the window.

"What the hell have I done wrong now?"

He turns his head all the way to look at me.

"Let it go."

"Why should I let it go?"

"Because you're not going to buy anything here. You understand. You're not buying anything."

"Oh, that's great. That's real nice. I offer my kids a few bucks to have a good time and I'm trying to buy them."

"What do you want from me, Dad? You want something?"

"I don't want a goddamn thing."

"Oh yeah you do. Yeah you do. You want us to say what a great guy you are and how everything's all right and you never fucked us up or scared the shit out of us or pissed our lives away."

He sits up.

"That's what you want, Dad. That's what you fucking want."

I throw the money halfway across the room at him. It lands on the floor.

"I don't want a goddamn thing from you."

He screams, "Keep your fucking money!"

I hear Bridget's door opening, but no footsteps.

I'm cornered and what comes up when I'm cornered is the rage—my whole body tenses in odd curves and my voice gets very loud and metallic. I get possessed. It's scary, I know. I've used it before. I'm screaming, and my eyes are filled with the scream.

"Fucking grow up, all right? All right? Fucking whine at somebody else. All right? You fucking sad-ass piece of shit. Cause I don't need it. All right? Cause I don't fucking need it."

Steve is off the couch, like a spring.

"Suppose I just punch your face in, old man. How about that? How about I punch your fucking old-man face in?"

"Come on, come on, let's go. You think you can, I'll kick your ass. I'll shut you up but good."

He stares at me and, God help me, I can see him as a little boy. He must have watched me do this as a little boy. *Oh God help me.*

"You're not worth my time," he says. "You haven't changed all that much." He walks right by me and through the kitchen. "You're still a lying, fucking drunk."

I hear Bridget's door close behind him. I'm standing there with froth on my lips and my fists balled. I go to the front door and open it and just stand there. I need to get away, but where can I go?

What did I say to him? What did I call him? Where do I get off with that shit? It's all in me like a cell-to-cell linked poison. It's all there. The real rage, the fake rage, the false pride, the self-pity, deep, deep resentments, self-justification, self-centeredness, and the willingness to say anything, do anything, to slip responsibility. What have I done?

Bridget comes out and stands behind me, a few feet away. "He's really hurting, Dad. You better talk to him."

How can I do that? He's seen me and heard me. How can I ever do that?

I walk back toward her room, trying not to put things together in my head, so maybe I can just talk. I can't talk about feelings. I can talk about love, gratitude, or resentment, but talking about love with my own son so it doesn't sound like a con—I can't do that. Everything I've learned, everything I've been, I picked up very early as defense. I picked it up from the carny guys at the arcade in Forest Park Highlands. I picked it up from a world of necessity.

Steve is sitting on the edge of the bed. I stand in the doorway.

"I think," I say, "that maybe you don't want a father right now." There's a silence. "Whenever you feel like you do, I'll be here." Pure patronizing noblesse oblige. "You know that, Steve. I love you and I'll be here."

He sighs and gets up and slides past me in the doorway. I left the front door open, so I don't hear him leave. Bridget is still in the living room. "I'm going out for a while," she calls.

I just stand there.

When the phone rings, I'm lying on the couch where Steve had been. It's late twilight. I haven't moved much at all.

"Yeah."

"It's over, Dad."

"What?"

"It's over. It's out and done. I don't feel it anymore."

What do I say? I don't say anything.

"It all got out and maybe we can just pick things up from a different place."

"That would be good."

"Yeah. It's over."

The phone clicks dead and I put it down. Over for him.

It's good, it is. But me? I see myself standing tense and curled in the middle of the living room frothing, screaming, threatening my son who never wanted a goddamn thing but my love. He was right. I haven't changed at all.

"Please take it away. Please God, take it away," I say, with tears in my eyes, not quite running. "Oh please help me; please, take it. Please help me. Jesus take the pain. Christ almighty I can't stand it. God, it's my whole life. God, please help me take it away. For God's sake, take it away. I can't stand it. I can't stand it. I ask you. I beseech You."

Chapter Eight

Made a list of all persons we had harmed,
and became willing to make amends to them all.

I won't know where to stop, once I start figuring out who I've harmed. I'm sure there are parking lot attendants I treated badly while drunk. I'm sure there are guys sitting in bars right now who remember me vaguely, remember some abuse or put-down. I wasn't always Jack the Glad Hand. Most of the time. Most of the time.

And I am willing to make amends to them all, already. I'd be happy to. I like the Step. It's "make a list and look at it; then do what you can."

I'm a lot more worried about the previous Steps.

I'm worried about my soul.

It's not something I've thought about all that much before, but I do as I move through the Steps. They don't come out clean, not completely, and as I look at how my life is going and what I'm doing and what I think I'm doing, it's begun to seem

to me that not only do I have two voices in my head, but neither of them is entirely trustworthy.

(*I stood in a bar bathroom once and almost saw the face
of the other. I heard his voice and he was saying, "Do it.
Drink it." And I drank it, went back to my coffee at the bar,
and looked up into the nowhere eyes of a clown painted on
velvet.*)

*Like the man said at the meeting, "I wanted to save my ass;
then I found out it was attached to my soul."*

The lines in the book haunt me—"those who are consti-
tutionally incapable of being honest with themselves.
They are not at fault. They seem to have been born that
way." *What if that's who I am down there?*

*This is the kind of Step I need, because I have to be sure I'm
doing something right. I need to establish my honesty with pen
and paper. I need it. I'll number the lines and I'll get every
name down that's still in my head.*

*I tell TK I'm worried about how thoroughly the Steps are
in me, how well I've worked them and taken them in, and
though he doesn't laugh at me, he could. It's good he doesn't because I'm not good at being laughed it.*

"*We claim spiritual progress, Jack, rather than perfection.
You ever hear that at a meeting? What? Are you special?
Who are you, King Drunk? Did you take the First Step all
right?*"

"*Yeah.*"

"*Then you're stuck with them, aren't you? There's no
going back. Doesn't matter where you are in the Steps, you'll*

be working them the rest of your life. Anybody you know doesn't?" TK says.

I hate being told I'm a schmuck.

~ ~ ~

THERE'S STEVE, OF COURSE. My focus tends to be on Steve because he's the oldest and he was just a little boy when the feelings started in me, the agony, the sense that I couldn't give him anything and that he'd be lost, just like me. There he was alone in the school yard and my heart would kick in my chest and my head would writhe. Then, I'd go to the bar and sit there, looking in the mirror.

I thought it was all the pain of being human, and some of it was, but mostly it was the pain of being a drunken, sentimental asshole (as in wanting to feel without taking responsibility). And I could see my own drunkenness haunting my little boy's eyes, hemming him into the school yard with haunted nights, agonizing blocked tears, and helpless, fugitive responsibility. (What did I do? What can I change?)

So my mind goes straight to Steve. But then, of course, there's Dave and Bridget too, and maybe I don't know as much about them because the mechanism's probably a little different for the second and third. Who knows? What do I know? They're sweet kids, but they don't show me much of what's in there.

"Hey kids," Daddy says, "let me see some of your pain, huh? I know I did it to you, but now I need you to feel some of the pain again so I can get better."

And there's Mom, of course, that good woman sitting in the St. Louis church like a wavering candle for the Virgin. Jack calling at two in the morning threatening to slash his wrists in a phone booth. Jack looking for money. Jack in her memory—a hopeful, sad little boy, hoping with her—stumbling through his life now like a vaudeville drunk and only touching base to drain her, to suck on her money and heart.

And Sarah, my ex-wife. I don't look too closely at Sarah because I've got that script in my head already and I'd rather not have to change it. Our mutual drinking, our mutual responsibility. Maybe she didn't stay out all night drinking and getting laid and spending all the money, but she did drink, didn't she? And she did get vicious—Jesus, she tried to run me down. So I'll make an amend but I won't overdo it.

My father? My father's dead. And better off.

I guess he loved me, and sometimes it showed. It was wonderful being with him then, just once in a while. I can't think of an amend to make because I didn't do anything to him. He's not alive anyway. All I can do is say in my head, "Hey, Dad. I got sober." (I could say, "I forgive you and all I care about is that you did love me, sometimes, and that you tried as best you could." I could say that, but where would it leave me?)

Chapter Eight

What else? My sister, the years of secret resentment and the impositions on her husband and her new life; the sundry professors I conned and cheated; Barbara Landau, the girl in the Village who nursed me; the bosses I ripped off, the work undone, the people who bought the doubtful properties I sold and the doubtful stocks; Jeannie who waited for me to marry her, who had to abort our child because I wasn't there for her to insist that she not; X, Y, and Z, and the shallow, stupid things I said to them in bars that helped them stay where they were on their stools; everyone I ever touched who was young and thought I was a pretty admirable guy, every one of them.

My mind slides around in the images, and I know I better just make a list fast or I'm going to start qualifying, evading, taking the easier way.

I'm haunted by the fact that it feels a little like Steve made amends *to me*—that he had no amends to make but called me up and said, "It's all over; it's gone." That somehow he had found that in himself and that it had made me feel better and grateful.

Why? Because his simple emotional honesty showed me up in a crummy, garish light? He wanted to beat the shit out of me and he could have. Why didn't he? I'm uneasy with the idea that he's come to terms with something that I don't completely feel yet, something that's just in my head.

Life is going on all around me, and somehow I'm in

it, but these Steps are going on too, and the one casts a light on the other, back and forth, and every bit of fear or anger, every misstep, makes my head quiver a little as I try to see in Step-light. The world is around me like a dioramic vodka ad, and walking through it is active fright—has been since I left Duffy's—so everything that happens is a threat unless I can make sense of it in the Steps. Sometimes I can; sometimes I have to sit down and wait till the fear passes.

One of the things you find out in the program is that there's a *physical* feeling of unity that comes with understood truth and that it's easily distinguishable from the self-justifications and the bullshit. It's an odd feeling—as if the soul were more deeply of the body than the mind is.

When things feel like they're just in your head, the only thing you can do is wait. Maybe it's going to take a disaster; maybe you'll just be walking down the street and catch an angle of sunlight and things will settle down into your gut. All you can do is keep doing what you're supposed to be doing—working the Steps and sorting the anxiety as it comes up. "Okay, this one is made of anger, resentment, and some old fear, abandonment maybe, maybe being helpless and about to be killed." So I sort and work at it, but not as well as I'd like.

I feel that I need to look at Sarah again and I don't want to.

Chapter Eight

The way the women in Sausalito used to look askance at her because she was Sarah, from Kansas, and dressed it. The way she tried to please me on our honeymoon with fancy lingerie and how I cut her down, hurt her, because it wasn't *my* fantasy, *my* pretense.

Sarah on the floor in the dark with blazing eyes, where I'd thrown her, having thrown the mattress on the floor with her on it. Sarah plucked from Kansas and stuck in shallow ground here—shallow, broken, shifting ground.

I try to hide but I can't, and once you put a name down on a list of people you need to make amends to, you're never going to be free until you see the whole thing clearly, the whole wretchedness.

Is this the way it's going to be for all my life? These nightmares and regrets washing over me at random? Could be. What do I know? They tell me that things get better and I have no reason to disbelieve.

Outside of my utter unwillingness to believe anything anybody has ever told me, my arrogance, my narcissism and rage, my "fuck you very much" attitude, and my fear of being weak, of being *seen*—I have no reason to disbelieve.

Should I make an amend to TK for thinking he would spread my Fifth Step around the program? Should I make an amend to the priest for using the confessional and sacrament to cover my ass and keep my sins from getting out?

My head goes in, my head goes out, and it turns my spirit to sauerkraut.

Life goes on, as I said, and while it does, these are the things of the spirit, the soul, the new world that go on in parallel, right below the surface. If it weren't for the meetings where there's suddenly number and substance, and my head isn't alone anymore, and I can take a hand to say a prayer without thinking about it, I don't know what I'd do.

The rooms are full of easiness. Sometimes the stories are so clear and harrowing that they're almost unbearable. Except for the number and the substance. (Where two or more are gathered together in my name.)

Sometimes they're light as air and human in the best possible way, in the playful light of easy spirits. Sometimes they're nothing at all but me and my head in a hard chair with a cup of lousy coffee. Sometimes they're all I have in this world, and I barely deserve them.

And every once in a while, I can talk to someone, a newcomer, and say something easy, something unpremeditated, and *mean it,* as in "I love you for no reason but this: that you're human and drunk and here."

Making my list is a solitary thing. Who's going to see it? Who's going to know?

Without a drink, the world is laid out on all sides and I have no direction except what's right, what rustles in my head and says "Right." Every emotion I ever sank is coming back up, dripping. There's a whole line of them trailing away under the water. They climb out onto the shore and wide landscape. "Hey Jack, remember me?"

I extend my right hand, and it's taken by the left hand of a kid, maybe nineteen, and my left hand is held by the right hand of a big guy who looks a little like Victor McGlaglen. My hands are holding theirs as well, and "Our Father," we say, "who art in heaven."

All alone in the afternoon light, I pick up the telephone and start. I won't start with the names at the top of my amends list, Christ no; I'll get my feet wet with the names on the bottom, the less serious cases.

The line of clambering, dripping emotions is moving past me on my right, taking up places on the dry ground. The light is unsteady, and the shadows creep.

So let me tell you now about the dry drunk.

A dry drunk is when you have all the emotions, all the physical pain and disorientation, and all the hideous solitude you had before, when you were drunk, but you don't have the alcohol to make it go away, so your nerves start screaming and trying to figure out what's going on.

It can come on quickly or slowly, but it always hits like a locomotive. I've read in Abraham Maslow's *The American Alcoholic* about a guy who woke up so totally racked with a hangover and withdrawal that he seized and died. He'd been sober for three months at the time.

I've been told about dry drunks, but I haven't really experienced one. At best, my life is a certain level of gray-sky depression softened by the faith I get every night at the meetings that I'm not drunk and I don't have to drink today. There are patches of blue sky but they close up quickly. This is enough, for now. I have a number of jumbled, conflicting motives and any number of flashes of alcoholic regret, resentment, and need, but essentially, compared with what I had before, I'm in a kind of heaven. It wouldn't be much to a non-drunk. Heaven wouldn't be the word that would come to their minds, but to me—living day to day without self-loathing at the end of any of them because I got drunk, waking up in the morning able to look at the day with a certain level of steadiness—heaven is not far off the mark. I may look at the day before me and see myself as a self-willed, ignorant, pushy, myopic asshole, but it's better. "We claim spiritual progress rather than spiritual perfection."

I'm there by the telephone and something is creeping in me. The light has become unpleasant and I feel like I need to be away from where I am but can't think of a single place to go. I have no place to go. There's this room and the meetings and the outside, which is nothing but one of those cardboard, Buck Rogers cities we used to put together on the floor with tabs and inserts. Things are getting flatter, so that when I turn my head suddenly, it's disorienting, the depths are off, and nothing is quite the same. This is a very subtle effect, but it doesn't take much spatial distortion to create vertigo.

I get up from the chair and the room is a flimsy, shoddy thing. I can do what now? I have so few things I do. Why would I read a paper? Everything in it is foretold and boring. I could get a cup of coffee, but I can feel it coursing in me and putting that caffeine edge in my head like a thin and wheedling voice. If I walk forward, I'll be at the wall. The house is empty, and whom do I want to talk to anyway?

It was easy enough being (no it wasn't) with a bottle like a Christmas present, looking at it with the expectation of going somewhere else, sitting down smoothly, with a glass (no it wasn't).

I'm so scared of that bottle, I could cry, but I can't stop to cry because every cell in me is saying "do something." And there's nothing to do. I'm a hollow man. I'm a collection of nerves and I've never done anything right, and now I'm blowing the only chance I have because I can't bear to *be*. I can't stand it.

My shirt is on my back, my pants are hanging, my shoes have my feet held in with no air at all, and my face is a great, fleshy, unbearable *thing* I carry in front of me. I'm jangled but my reflexes are gone and that's terrifying in itself because I can feel it. If something happened suddenly, I couldn't handle it, and if I were blindsided (and all I've got are blind sides), I'd go down hard.

I don't know what I need. It isn't that I crave alcohol. It's just that I don't think my nausea will ever stop. Booze isn't available to take it away like it used to. I'm just a goddamn thing, dropped where I am, and no one in the world knows where I am and couldn't care less because I'm broken, a throwaway. If it weren't for the terror, this would be self-pity; if it weren't for the weight of my body, it would be the end of my mind.

I have a body, still, and it has just enough weight to hold me down, keep my feet on ground. I need to make it heavier, so I go out to the kitchen and get a box of Entenmann's chocolate donuts and eat them one at a time, leaning over the kitchen table that is much too white, too glaring. I eat them all and it helps while I'm chewing but when they're all gone, the great spaces open up behind me again and I'm afraid to turn around.

Can I drive?

No.

I need to drive. I need to go see TK.

What does driving mean?

It means thousands of pounds of jagged steel hurtling by, each with a separate mind guiding, each with someone else's mind on the wheel. The roaring of the traffic, the judgments to be made, the tearing steel at sixty-five, controlled by minds, each with their own madness.

I go out front and get in the van. I go back in the

house and make a peanut butter sandwich and eat it. I'm like a hot-air balloon with too few sandbags. I go back to the van and turn the key in the ignition. I pull away from the curb like a kid on a tricycle. I'll go see TK.

I get out on the freeway without any problems, but my palms are sweating. The freeway is streaming and I'm not sure I can merge. But I do. Then there's the sounds going by, voices, and I can't make them out but they're streaming by me and my hands are slipping on the wheel. When I get to the off-ramp, it's a little better because I can see more clearly; things aren't moving too fast; but my gas-pedal leg is starting to tremble, so I stop in Mill Valley at a Kentucky Fried Chicken place and sit in the van getting greasy while I eat as fast as I can.

Then I get back on the road. Three blocks from Tom's house, I stop at Baskin Robbins and buy three prepackaged ice-cream sandwiches and eat them as I drive. I haven't called Tom, so he may not be home.

But he is. *God, thank you.* When he opens the door, he says, "Jesus, Jack, you're white as a sheet."

"I'm not too well today."

He offers me coffee but that's the last thing I need. He sits me in a big living room chair. I look around the room and it's less jangling than mine was at home. It has some depth.

"I guess this is a dry drunk," I say.

"Well, what's going on?"

I tell him. I want to know what I'm doing wrong.

"You're not doing anything wrong. Dry drunks happen."

"What do I do?"

"What you're doing."

"I'm not doing anything. I'm scared."

"You're in a dry drunk. Everybody is scared in a dry drunk."

That's it? I wish I had someone to hold me, but I don't think my skin would react well; I think it would be electric and unpleasant.

"This is going to happen no matter how hard you're working the program. It wouldn't be as bad, maybe, if you had some simple faith, but essentially, everybody gets it, some worse than others."

"I have faith."

"You have faith you think about. If it's filtered through your head, it's not as reliable as it might be. You need it in your gut." He smiles a little. "Or maybe you prefer the Colonel's chicken."

I have no sense of humor. "I made my list, my Eighth Step."

"Changing the subject?"

I don't say anything.

"Look Jack, you think you're a secret but you're not. Anyone who's been sober for a couple of years can see right through you. It's okay; you'll get there. But if you keep trying to work the program in your head, you're going to have more trouble than you need. Everybody knows, Jack. Most everybody's been there."

This is oddly comforting, that they can see through me. I guess because even though they can, they haven't turned away.

I'm coming down.

"Tell me about your list. How many worthless pricks are you willing to forgive for letting you fuck them over?"

He makes me smile a little.

Chapter
Nine

Made direct amends to such people wherever possible,
except when to do so would injure them or others.

*This could mean paying debts, on top of everything else. I'm
okay with money for a bit, but I'm afraid—I don't feel secure
at all. (When was I ever secure?)*

*It could also mean humiliation, which I'm not good at. I'm
pretty good at humiliating myself—I was—but I'm not good at
consciously giving people the power to do it to me.*

*Or it could mean getting punched in the mouth, abused in
public, cut deeply, or hurt in a way I couldn't stand.*

*But then again there's the possibility that I'll get my head
free for the first time since I was a kid. I'll have to start again,
of course; I'll have to sit down in the chair with the phone, my
list, and actually dial a number.*

*"Hi," I'll say. "This is Jack Erdmann" (those will be the
relatively easy ones—the ones that begin "Hi, this is Jack," will
be something else again). "You may not remember me but . . ."*

I think they'll remember me.

The Eighth Step doesn't say "those we had harmed impor-tantly"; it says "all persons we had harmed." I don't know yet that the most important ones are the ones who will feel per-mitted to forgive because I've asked.

I don't know a lot of things, but at least I'm good with the phone. What the hell else have I been doing all these years but working the phone (lying on the phone). This will tap into my skills differently—no lies.

~ ~ ~

THE ASTONISHING THING is that I'm sober and it's starting to settle into me. I wake up in the morning and I can find plenty of fear and anxiety but no misery, horror, or intrinsic worthlessness. My life is going on as always, but I have a life inside the Steps too, and that life is firming up the other.

I wake up feeling like a human being in a world of human beings. I wake up knowing that while I may be weak, flimsy, resentful, self-serving, and scared, I'm still a reasonably decent human being and that up and down the block are other humans who feel much the same way. They may look at themselves and cringe, but then they put on their clothes and face the day.

The savagery of my need for alcohol has backed off, though it still hits at odd times. It's still stronger than I am, in many ways. But it's not there pulling me in. I don't hear that fearful voice say, "Whether you drink or not doesn't matter because you are just as afraid of not drinking as you are of drinking, so it makes no difference, does it? The only way out of this mess is a drink."

Now the urge to drink is intermittent, an occasional fist in the face, an occasional weakness at the knee. The occasional dry drunk. (Never again, please.)

At the meetings are all these sets of eyes looking back at me. All of them share the same information. Most of them are kind. Most of them have done the Steps (although they tell me the Steps don't end, I still think they've done them and that's why they're at peace in ways I'm not), and they're not surprised at anything that comes into the room.

AA has heard it all.

(Sometimes there's an edge of irritation in me, when I *feel* that, when I suddenly feel that my life has been a cookie-cutter affair with "drunk" spelled out in icing.)

The days have gotten shorter and twilights harder. There's always a creeping edge of sadness and fear at twilight. Other people sit down with a martini before dinner. The thought fills me with more fear than the twilight. Mill Valley is dark with redwoods. They can be oppressive and the twilight hangs in them as if it were draped there. What are you going to do now, the twilight asks? You're all alone in the dark and it's getting darker. What's it going to be like when you're trying to fill the hours, when the television doesn't work anymore and the lights are out in most of the house?

Steve and Bridget are back from Europe. They had a great time and Steve doesn't particularly want to talk about it and Bridget only talks in general terms ("It was wonderful"). Both of them are out most of the time or off in their rooms. Dave has moved in, but he's seldom around. Dave is a musician with all that implies. I'm around. The house is full of Erdmann at six, Erdmann at thirteen, Erdmann and Erdmann and Erdmann. I have to plan how an evening will be sometimes, then not deviate. Once I get through the twilight, there's a meeting (merciful God) and then when I get back, I turn on the light in my room, hang up my jacket, leave the light on, sit in the big chair, and turn on the television to look for some reasonably paced, professional movie with tension and explosions. I put my feet up. I pick up an unread section of newspaper I had left next to the chair before I went to the meeting. I take care of the little things, as best I can, because I'm not capable of taking care of the big things. My nerves aren't whole yet, and neither is my mind. I heard a guy at a meeting say that the biggest things in his getting sober were brushing his teeth and combing his hair every morning. He said that twenty-four hours sober, he'd gone into a store and bought a toothbrush and outside he'd started to cry because it felt like the bravest, best thing he'd ever done. Just to presume that there might be some reason to brush his teeth made him happy.

I barely remember the time that's passed since I stopped drinking. I remember meetings though. I remember where I'm safe.

On a Tuesday morning, I finish my coffee and sit down to think about my list, to really look at it. The best place to start, I think, is at the liquor store where kindly Charlie kept me going with a supply of food. Charlie's at Colonial Liquors, which is right across the street from the basement apartment where I sank into terror and vilified my son. I can still smell it all—the sourness, the old, knotted sheets, the dampness in the basement, the empties, the moldy food. I can smell myself, sweating, the fine edge of acid coming off my skin. I can taste the vodka, cold out of the freezer in the little refrigerator, and warm from where I hid bottles in bushes, piles of old clothes, under the hood of the van, next to the battery, inside the knotted sleeve of an old coat in the closet.

Pretty soon I'll have been sober for a year. Doesn't feel like it, sometimes. If I didn't have the meetings, I'd shake myself to death.

So I'll get in the van and go over to the big, bright turn in the road where the apartment is, and the Colonial, and each memory up and down the street like a station of the cross.

Oh, yeah. Right there was the phone booth that the fire department had to cut me out of.

I stole from Charlie, even though he was probably the only real friend I had then. I stole from him because he had the liquor and I didn't. Once, I got down on my knees in the back of the store—the mirror didn't show the floor—and opened a bottle right there and took a hit because I couldn't wait till I hit the street. I couldn't make it.

I'd go in and pretend to chat because he had already said he wouldn't sell me any more booze. He would give me milk, eggs, and bread—then he'd turn around and I'd steal from him.

Charlie's behind the counter and I can tell he's surprised to see me. His smile makes me feel good. He must be guessing that I'm not the nightmare anymore, just a guy who's come to talk. And I explain and he says, "Jeez, Jack, you're not telling me anything new but thanks anyway, for thinking about me. You were pretty sick, you know?"

"Yeah, Charlie. I just wanted to let you know I remember what I did and how good you were to me. Let me pay you for—"

He waves one hand in the air. "Forget it, Jack. I have."

We stand around for a bit, but we don't have a lot to talk about beyond the old days. When I leave, I walk across the street I used to be afraid to try and cross—four lanes, traffic coming around a bend—and stand looking at the street-level windows on the long dark space I'd lived in all those broken, sinister months. I don't bend down or anything; I just look, hands in pockets.

Up Sir Francis Drake, to the left, is the fire department. I think about it, shrug, and start walking. I can be suddenly astonished in the street that I'm able to walk, that I'm capable, and that my feet fit the ground. People come toward me and pass and I don't see any shift of the eye, like "Oh God, let him go by."

The sun is shining and I can walk and other people aren't afraid to see me. I'm grateful.

"I'm the guy you cut out of the phone booth," I say to the guy in the open garage door.

He looks at me. "Jesus Christ. Hey, Tommy! Look who's here."

Tommy comes out of the back. I've never seen either of them before. "Well you sure look different," Tommy says.

"Just came by to say thank you and apologize for what I put you through."

"Hell, it was good for telling stories. You know you're the only guy we ever cut out of a booth?"

"They never put it back, just hauled it away," Tommy says.

"I don't drink anymore."

What a stupid thing to say.

"Good for you, good for you. One less drunk to call in the middle of the night, huh Tom?"

"You got it."

"Well, thanks again."

"You were really in there. You had this goddamn crowd and everyone had advice on how to do it. Good to see you. Take it easy."

Walking away is tough. My head is twisting around—I can feel them behind me, watching. I walk across the street and eat a burrito at the little Mexican place on the corner. Then I walk up the path into the College of Marin grounds, but it's much too lively with sweet-young-thing college girls and light through the trees and low voices making plans. What am I here for anyway? The van is way the hell back by the Colonial. I sit on a bench for a minute, then head back. I'm watching myself do all this stuff.

Driving away from the big bend in the road, I feel pretty good. Two for two. I set out to do it and I did it. Two for two and no humiliation.

I call up TK and tell him what I've done. "Great, Jack," he says, "and when you get to the tough ones, call me first."

I call my sister.

"I prayed for you every day, Jack."

In some obscure way, I don't want to hear that. Pat is still the devout little girl, sailing right past my father's brutality without a care in the world, poised and prim on her goody two-shoes.

"I guess it worked."

"It always will. You were remembered in hundreds of masses. You always were a good Catholic, Jack. You just didn't know it, sometimes."

Why does this bother me so much? I thank God in the street, walking. I thank God I've got through another day, at its end, in the dark. It's the Catholic part—it's the Church. I believed them. I was a terrified little kid and I believed them, but nothing came back to me. Then I had to sit with my father as he cried, slobbered, and asked me to pray to the Virgin for him. It wasn't fair. It's amazing how deeply the sharp edge to "it wasn't fair" can cut. A child's sense of injustice is a terrible, powerful thing. All I found in the Church was wine in the sacristy.

"Is Barbara there?" I say. Barbara is my niece. I called once from a motel in Nevada and only she was home and I must have scared the living hell out of her, telling her to tell her mother that I was going to kill myself with a steak knife against my belly in the sad-ass motel light.

"Barbara?"

"Yes."

"This is your Uncle Jack and I just wanted to tell you that I'm *so* sorry for having scared you on the phone when I was drunk."

Pause. "That's all right, Uncle Jack; we all love you."

"The hell we do," I hear in the back. It's Karl, Pat's husband. I stole most all the liquor from his cabinet.

"He was a jack-off when I met him and he's still a jack-off," says Karl.

I put the tip of my tongue between my lips.

"Could I talk to your father, hon?"

"Uh, Dad, Uncle Jack wants to talk to you."

"Yeah, what is it this time, Jack?"

"I wanted to say I'm sorry. I wanted to let you know I'm sorry for stealing from you and I'm sorry for all the chaos I caused and—"

"Do you know what you put Pat through? Do you have any damn idea what you put her through? The best damn thing you can do, Jack, is stay the hell out of her life. You're a goddamn waste of her time, and that's a fact."

"I'm sorry, Karl."

"Well I'm all impressed to hell—"

Pat takes the phone back.

"The feelings are still raw, Jack. Karl doesn't mean what he says."

"The hell I don't," he yelled in the background.

"You were prayed for every day."

"I know. Thank you. Thank you."

"God forgives you, Jack, so how could we not?"

"Thank you."

"Mom is the one who really suffered and she prayed for you too."

"Yeah."

When I hang up, I'm a little shaky and I still have

an edge of thanklessness in my head. First there's the Church and then there's Karl. What did the Church ever do for me? The hell with Karl with his six or seven bottles of booze he never even opened because he didn't have enough imagination to have a few. Screw him.

I call up TK.

"That's the way it goes," he says. "When it's going to be tough, you should give me a call."

"Yeah, I should have. Jesus."

"Yeah, some folks just won't get their throats off your knife, will they?"

"Oh."

"Yeah, 'oh.'"

"Yeah. He never had any reason to like me."

"Sometimes you have to duck. So duck. But don't think you've got any complaints coming. Did Karl make you steal his liquor?"

"Nah."

"Does he love his wife?"

"Yeah."

"Did you make her miserable and scared for a long time?"

"Yeah."

"'Jack-off' is probably a pretty good description."

So I'm back in my big chair at square one. Not really. It just feels that way for a while as the past comes washing back in bits and pieces. Pat and I are just a couple of kids in a house with a blithe Catholic chorus girl and a drunken piano player. How did she know how to float the way she did? How did she know?

(She didn't have to know anything. Dad never even threatened her, not once.)

Oh, the injustice. I look again at my list, let it fall to the floor, and go out to the kitchen for a cup of coffee. I stand there with the coffee, open the refrigerator, and take out a box of donuts. I eat them all. Might as well be on the safe side.

Harley, my last boss, is on the list. I ripped him off up and down, but maybe this one I can do by mail. So I get myself a couple of sheets of paper. "Dear Harley . . ."

I write three sheets and look at them, read them over, and realize that I'm a lot better on the page than I am on the phone. Why should that be? The phone is my medium. (For what?)

But in the letter I've managed to cover it all—what I did, how I feel—and show even an edge of gratitude for the way he put up with me in the last days. It's pretty good. If I'd called him, what would I have said? Maybe there are times for one approach and times for another. I put a stamp on the envelope and walk down to the mailbox.

I need to talk to the kids, of course, and Sarah, and Jeannie.

There was another woman too; who was she? I remember a woman with graying hair and she took me to her house in the afternoon and her little boy was there and some other people came by and they put me to bed. Where was that? Why did they put me to bed? I don't know and never will. I sit back and look toward the window. How many others are there?

The various women in the bars, the cab drivers, the cops, the guys at Lincoln House, the staff at the crisis unit (no, that's the guy who beat the shit out of me while I was tied down), the staff at the loony bin in Reno, staffers everywhere, especially volunteers. Madness.

First things first. I'll talk to my kids, one at a time, of course.

Steve will be okay because he's already said it—that it's all gone—so it won't be hard. Bridget is a sweetheart and so she'll be okay. Dave was always kind of on my side anyway and hated it when Sarah threw me out. Maybe I'll have to explain that she had every reason to throw me out. He knows that. How could he not? So I think it won't be bad.

(Is that how to approach this? To set it up so it won't be bad?)

I have it in my head that the way to do it is to be sitting outside in the van with each, talking, while looking out the windshield. That's how I see the picture.

(What the hell is that? I'm still Jack the missing father, coming by to explain it all to the kids, then hitting the road again.)

I ask Steve to come out with me and he looks a little

strange but does it. He sits there behind his glasses, looking out the windshield. When I'm finished, he says, "I don't have to hear any of this. It isn't necessary and I don't want to go back anymore."

And I get Bridget out there and she barely lets me get started before she goes into a kind of shock and says, "Don't say anything, okay? Don't say anything."

And Dave comes out and cries. I'm astonished because he's not the one I would have thought had tears to shed.

(How much do I know about my own children? How much time have I given them? It's easy to figure. All I have to do is deduct the drinking time from the whole married life.)

I'm sitting in the van calling them out as if we're back in Tahoe and Sarah hasn't let me in. Sarah's still in Tahoe in our house. And how does she feel? She drinks. How will that go? Do I want to park the car and walk across the deck, up to the door, through the door to where Sarah will be with maybe a drink in her hand and the old savage light in her eyes? Can I do it by phone? By letter?

(Hell no.)

I still think she has a lot of responsibility in what happened. I mean she was drunk too. Will she make amends?

(She isn't sober, why should she?)

Am I supposed to try to get her to stop drinking?

(Don't even give it a thought.)

What will I say?

("Hi Sarah, I came to say I'm sorry for the nineteen years.")

I call up TK the following morning and tell him how I feel and he says, "Fine. Tell you what. I'll drive you up and back, just for support. But I can't do it till Friday."

Friday sounds fine. Friday may never come.

Friday comes and we drive way the hell up to Tahoe, and I sit in the front seat remembering every rest stop, every restaurant, every disaster, every grief, delusion, and resentment.

It turns out to be pretty simple. I call up Sarah and she says, "Fine, come on over," and over we go. She isn't drinking when we go in, but is in no time. Vodka over ice, as she chats it up with TK. I try to think what should happen next.

"You think we could have a talk, Sarah? Maybe we could take a little walk and let Tom unwind?"

She looks at me, her eyes a little vodka-bright. "Oooh, I suppose."

I get up and she does too, a lot more slowly than I, unwinding from the chair, and then suddenly we're out on the deck. It's winter in Tahoe and there I am again with the log going through the window and Sarah hating me with every fiber of her being.

"I've got a lot to apologize for," I say. "I—"

She's walking down the stairs to the driveway. "I don't want to hear it."

"I—"

She looks back at me from the bottom of the stairs. "I don't want to hear it."

"I talked to the kids and—"

"I don't want to hear it, Jack. I don't want to hear any of it."

"But—"

"No buts. I don't care and I don't want to hear it." She takes a sip of her drink. "It's dead and that's how it's going to stay."

"Okay."

"So it was a long drive for nothing if that's why you made it."

"No, it wasn't the whole thing."

"Well good, because I don't want to hear it."

"Sure."

She stands on the deck as Tom and I drive away. She waves once, then turns.

"Sorry I dragged you all the way up here for nothing," I say.

"It wasn't nothing," says TK.

"It wasn't much."

"Did you do what you had to do?"

"I guess."

"Okay then."

Chapter
Ten

Continued to take personal inventory and when
we were wrong promptly admitted it.

*I don't feel like I need to take a personal inventory. I feel like
everyone I see is doing it for me, like that son-of-a-bitch in the
corner who keeps looking at me and rapping his fingers on the
table.*

*Which is what I've been defending against all my life: keep-
ing them out of the secret place where I'm crying with fright and
it's always 1933. I'm always trying to be loved but don't know
how to be different than I am and there's something so wrong
with me that even my father can't love me, even my father.*

*This is not the core of a man who says he's wrong, who says
he's sorry. This is the core of a man who'll explode if you get
anywhere near him, near it.*

*This is the core of a smiling, unconcerned, glad-hand drunk
who thinks what he has is pride. Because he never felt the real*

*thing. Or maybe felt it sometimes ("Look what I did, Dad")
but backed away from the angry eyes, floundering, looking for
the door.*

What's a personal inventory anyway?

*Do I have to wake up in the morning and say, "Well, you
look like shit this morning and the job you had is over and
you've conned another woman into your bed (I didn't,
did I?). You're scared, shaky, and if you stay like this, you're
just going to be Jack-without-a-drink" and that's no good
at all.*

*I'm still making amends, of course. So that's good, but
something is bloody missing, and when it's late at night and
I'm just sitting looking stupidly at the television, I feel like I
should be doing something else. I have unfinished business. I
notice I look forward to going to sleep the way I used to look
forward to a drink. Now is this good or bad?*

*I don't think I should look forward to anything like I
looked forward to a drink. But what the hell, I'm in process,
and it feels all right, right now, to pull up the covers that way.*

*There are a few things you can say to yourself anytime that
will get you through. One is "I'm in process."*

*Another is "I'm doing my best." The best one is "I'm not
drunk." That one comes in the morning and brightens the
world as it starts to appear. If I'm not drunk, I can do anything. I believe that, and it scares me. What might I be asked to
do? Apologize? Say I'm wrong? I can do that, I can. All I have
to do is promptly recognize it when I'm wrong.*

Chapter Ten

Hell, it feels like I'm always wrong. I'll just sort out the obvious stuff.

~ ~ ~

THERE IS AN AMEND I haven't made and that's wrong. I don't want to do it because I can barely stand the thought of seeing Jeannie and saying, "Hi, sorry I didn't show up for the wedding."

I know she's better off because if I had married her, what would her life have become? But that doesn't matter because there she was, and all her relatives, and I left her alone—humiliated, mumbling excuses, covering for me, and exposed to the eyes of others turning away from her.

I'm wrong. I'm wrong. I'm the wrong guy.

I get in my VW van, which I hate, and head up to Reno to Marie Callender's restaurant, where Jeannie will be sitting in a booth along about two o'clock. "Keep it simple" is my mantra. If I can just not stumble and justify, maybe it'll be all right. For whom? For me. That's what I think because I don't quite realize yet that the person who forgives, the forgiver, gets more back than the forgivee.

The sweep of the road into Reno is just like always. I keep my head straight and watch the road. I pass the bend where I once slid down its bank in a sleeping bag.

I pass the road signs that used to point to hell. I pass the whole landscape as if it were some painted backdrop to the Jack Erdmann Story.

I'm not driving fast, not anymore, because the damn van won't go fast and lumbers up into the mountains as if I were pushing a wheelchair, not motoring a van.

These were the places of my heart all right—the grand mountains, rolling flatlands, the sodden sky in Reno with a pink cinderblock bar, the sad-eyed bartenders and angry cops. And the loony bin. The suspended animation.

(Let me get through this, God. I'll just stop, be quiet, and it will all go away.)

Somehow in the middle of the madness, I found Jeannie.

Well, I am sorry. I'm sorry I did it, though I was just being sensible, really, finding someone to take care of my extended dying.

"Drunks don't have relationships; they have hostages." God knows I've heard that often enough. How do I say to Jeannie, "Well, hon, you were just a hostage."

I don't. Of course I don't.

Jeannie's in the restaurant waiting as I walk through the sodden air to the door. It's dim at least, and cool. There she is at a table facing the big front window; her bright, striking face in a setting of black hair. Her eyes, ah, her eyes.

Chapter Ten

"Hi."

"Hello Jack. How have *you* been?"

I sit down. "I'm not drunk."

"So I see. That's something." She has a cup of coffee in front of her.

"Would you like lunch?"

"I have to get back to work. Sooner or later. So why did you call, Jack?"

"Yeah, coffee," I say to the waiter.

"Well what I did was terrible, and I know it. . . ."

"Most people would."

". . . and I needed to tell you how sorry I am—about the way things were and what I did."

"I lived."

"You didn't deserve that and . . ."

(What the hell. That's not a good thing to say.)

". . . I needed to tell you that you deserved a lot better than me, the way I was. I'm sorry, Jeannie. I didn't mean it, but I did it and can't run away."

"No? Neither could I. Just out of curiosity, where were you?"

"I was in detox."

"Detox. You should have let me know and I could have said to everyone, 'Oh, not to worry. Jack's in detox, and he'll be around again in a year or so.'"

"I just fell apart and it got worse when I got out because I couldn't stop."

"Do you know what it was like, Jack? I told everyone, 'I'm happy and I'm getting married and I want you to be happy for me too.' You know what that was like? When you didn't show, didn't call, and everybody had to pretend that nothing really bad had happened? 'Oh I'm sure it's nothing, Jean. He'll be calling. It's just one of those things, you know; he'll be calling.' Then they all kind of wander away and I have to go home and sit there? You know what that was like?"

"Yeah."

"No you don't." She throws two dollars on the table. "I'm glad you're sober, Jack. I think it's great for you. And I'm glad you said you're sorry, because you sure as hell should be. But I'm a working girl, you know, and I need to get back to my unimportant life."

She stands up with her eyes crackling. "You have a long ride back, and I need to get to work."

"Can you forgive me?"

"No," she says and walks out the door. What's to do? I sit there till I'm sure her car has left the lot, then get up and go back to my van and sit there for a while behind the wheel.

I can't go back with an eraser. God knows if I could, I'd erase this whole stinking town. That's a lousy thought. I just want to cover my tracks; I want to be in a world where no one remembers how I was, what I did, a world where I don't even remember.

I continue to take a personal inventory in the parking lots of the past. I rest my head briefly on the steering wheel, but then remember that every cop knows that pose of a worn-out drunk, and do I really need a cop now? With a little luck I'd get one who knows me.

Well, what the hell? I'll just zip over to Tahoe and tell Sarah all about this. "Hey Sarah, remember the woman I was seeing? I don't think you ever met her, but . . ." Sarah lives in the house I bought by the wonderful lake, where we were supposed to all be happy, surrounded by beauty, the sighing of the trees, and a cozy little town where all the drunks know each other and cluster together. We drunks then are good guys. What you did the night before is funny, really early in the morning, in the bar on the piers near the beautiful water the sun glares off. We're all good guys. It's a good man's failing.

"What did you do? You're kiddin' me? No shit, Jack, you're a madman. No shit? Jeez. I left at two and you were lookin' not so bad. Shit. Hey Harry, give me a brandy and coffee, huh? Light on the coffee. So what did she do, Jack? She call the cops?"

It's a good man's failing. It's an endless, sad-ass charade and hanging from each of us are tatters of past indecencies, expectations, dead hopes.

I pick up my head because I don't want to tell the cops that I haven't been drinking. I don't ever want to tell the cops anything, ever again.

(My heart jumps a little. The remembered black and

153

white in the mirror like a sudden giant bug on my shirt front.)

Four hours back to the city. I could have done this by phone, I guess, but it wouldn't have been right. At least Jeannie had the moment of getting up and walking out and leaving me sitting there. It must have felt good.

(In a lot of ways, I still know nothing at all.)

I'm down out of the mountains and into Sacramento, down 80 to 37, over to 101, and back to my driveway where I put my head on the wheel and sit there. What did I expect? I'm lucky she didn't throw her coffee in my face. I'm lucky she didn't really hurt me. She could have. She could have said a lot of things, loudly.

(Sex stuff, weakness stuff, money stuff, weepy-little-boy stuff.)

I'm lucky. But I have a lousy feeling in my chest, as if I were about to have a heart attack so I don't move at all, for ten minutes or so, breathing steady as I can. "Our Father," I say, "who art . . ." It's just the panic, the old psychotic, coming-down physical fear, the heightened everything, the flutter in the chest, the pressure coming up the arm, the "God this is it, no way to stop now" *present*.

I've been here before. I wait it out and continue. ". . . deliver us from evil."

I get out of the van like an old man. I'm carrying a sack of worn-out parts in my chest and my head is a

154

fluttering white flag. I go in and sit down and call TK, who tells me just what I knew he'd tell me. He's there to remind me when I forget.

"You get what you paid for, Jack, okay? You're doing what you need to do to not drink. And you didn't drink. In the long run, that's going to be your amend— that you don't drink and you're there for people."

When we were wrong promptly admitted it.

There's a difference, isn't there, between saying you're sorry for something you did while you were drunk and saying, "I'm wrong," in the present, as it happens? It's making amends on a twenty-four-hour basis. When I said to Jeannie, "You didn't deserve that," I should have stopped right there and said, "I was wrong to say that and I'm sorry. I patronized you and implied that you *could have* deserved it, that you might have." But that way lies madness.

Or does it? I could have done that. I mean what would have been the problem?

I don't want to be wrong. I was wrong all my life, but I had goddamn good reasons and I still have some. I'm just a human being and I'm not going to go around apologizing every ten minutes and boring the shit out of everybody. I remember John Wayne in *She Wore a Yellow Ribbon* saying, "Never apologize; it's a sign of weakness."

That's horseshit; I know that. But on the other hand, how many at meetings have said to me, "Sorry

Jack, that must have made you feel pretty bad. I was wrong to say that"?

None, that's how many.

How many said, "I was wrong to do that," when they didn't show up for the party I gave and never even called to let me know?

I get a cup of coffee (that's what I need all right; let's get the fluttery heart really moving) and sit down. I pick up the phone and call TK again.

"Yeah, Jack?"

"Look, I think I'm being reasonable here. I mean, I'm trying not to get into resentments, but I'm thinking about all the guys I know who treated me like shit early on in the program and I don't remember any of them saying, 'Hey, I was wrong and I admit it.' I don't remember any. What is it, just newcomer obligation?"

TK sighs.

"Jack, if another guy fucks up and acts like he isn't a drunk, does that mean you aren't a drunk?"

"No."

Silence.

"Are you allowed to do everything anyone else in the program does? You know how many guys go out and drink?"

"Yeah."

"Why do you want to be wrong, Jack?"

"What?"

"Why do you want to be wrong? If you don't want to

admit being wrong, then you want to be allowed to be wrong. Where's the payoff?"

Silence.

"I don't want to look weak."

"Is it easy to admit you're wrong?"

"No."

"Are you weak when you do difficult things?"

"No."

Silence.

"It's pride."

"It's false pride, Jack. It's false pride."

"Oh."

When I hang up, I think back to the things I made my pride out of, and I shudder. I never had any pride at all, not really. All I had was a defense that went with a face and an attitude, both of them based on fear and the feeling of being unloved, unlovable, and incompetent.

("I love you," said my wife. *Sure you do,* I thought, *sure you do—for now.*)

How proud was I when I was drinking from a bottle on my hands and knees on the floor at Colonial Liquors, stealing from the only friend I had who'd give me some eggs and bread?

I get up and throw the coffee in the sink. I can admit it when I'm wrong.

(Remember it's right now you're admitting; it isn't about the past.)

I can do that.

(Remember you couldn't be wrong because if you felt wrong and you went in front of your father that way, it would only be worse.)

I always felt wrong.

(Whom did you tell?)

The guys I had to deal with weren't in the program. The kids I grew up with weren't in the program. Hardly anyone in my life was in the program. I had to live in the real world, didn't I?

(Is that what you did?)

Oh Christ, give me a break. I look at the clock and it's 3:06. I look at it half an hour later and it's 3:08.

I go into the kitchen, open the refrigerator, and take out what seems to be about two pounds of leftover meat loaf that Suzie made. I have Suzie now, I think to myself, and what a sweetheart she is—intelligent, good-hearted, blond, pretty, and long-legged.

She is much more than I deserve. I have to stop saying that, TK tells me, because if I get used to saying the "much more than I deserve" stuff, feeling it, I'm right on the edge of throwing my respect away, again.

I met Suzie in the program and when I get back from this sweeping landscape of insomnia, I'll call her, we'll go have dinner, then curl up together, and everything will be fine.

I eat the leftover meat with my fingers, standing at the kitchen table. When I'm finished, I feel more real.

There are things I should be thinking about. Shelter

Chapter Ten

Bay is over and I need a new job fast. I'll make a list of the possibilities.

(Without list-making, the first year of sobriety would be even harder. I can make lists of anything at all and feel like I've accomplished something.)

I get out the paper, a pen, and sit down, but I can't stay down, so I get up again and take a shower, lost in steam, and come out thinking, Jeannie will come around when it sinks in. You did all right. Maybe I should call her and she'd back off a little and I wouldn't have to feel so guilty. "Leave it alone," TK had said. "Leave it alone." Is that what he said? I'm not calling again because I don't want to feel like a pest.

I have two sponsees of my own and one of them is new, from the meeting a couple of nights ago where I spoke ("I *really* like what you had to say and I wanted to ask if you'd be my sponsor"). He's a nice-enough guy, around thirty with a new divorce and a couple of lost, frightened kids and a couch to sleep on at a friend's house. He calls all the time. He calls before he crosses the street. Sometimes, when I'm lost myself, it's hard and I find I'm quoting things I've been told without the slightest involvement or comprehension because I can't *always* focus, can't shift my focus to Frank every time I pick up the phone and it's him. He has a mind that leaps from doubt to doubt like he's most afraid of *doing* something. Some days he's not sure he's an alcoholic; some days he's not sure that his wife really wants to divorce him; some days he thinks his "drinking problem" came from the tensions in the marriage; and some days he's intolerable. Then, I can't go around and around with him and his doubts, arranged in a circle.

"At least I'm not like that," I think, and then the phone rings and I answer it and it's Frank. He wants to know how he can *know* if he's taken the First Step. I tell him he's wasting his time worrying about it, that if he hasn't, it's going to come around again and bite him in the ass.

"So you don't think I should worry about it?"

"No, Frank, let it go."

Ten minutes later the phone rings again. I pick it up, thinking it's Jeannie, but it's Frank.

"I'm working the First Step again and I don't know how to do it, because I'm just not sure that my life is unmanageable and if it isn't, then I'm faking it."

"Are you a drunk, Frank? Do you want to drink now?"

"I don't think so."

"You don't think so?"

"Well, it looks like I am a drunk. I mean I got the DWIs; I got myself pretty deep into trouble, but that's what people do when things are tough, right? Sometimes they drink too much for a while."

"You call ten years a while?"

"Well some of it was just social drinking. I tell you,

Chapter Ten

Jack, I hear these people talking about how they can't drink ever again, and it doesn't *feel* like me. Just sometimes. Then I feel dishonest. I mean the First Step is a big deal."

"Read the stories in the Big Book."

"I did that."

"Read them again. Take my word, if nothing else. You've been drunk for ten years and half the bartenders and all the cops in Marin never want to see you again."

"You think it's that bad?"

"Yeah, Frank, that's what I think."

"I'll work on faith. Thanks, Jack."

The thing is that the guy really is in pain and that's the way his mind works; he can't help it, and he probably needs someone with a lot more sobriety than I've got but what can I do, he asked me, and I know that newcomers sometimes instinctively pick the one sponsor who won't be able to handle them because that's a slick way out and back to the bottle. "My AA sponsor didn't even give a shit," they whine. What can I do about it? I could ask Frank to find someone else, but I feel like maybe I'm supposed to; maybe I need to be the one.

(I look at everything that way. Is this or that what I'm supposed to be doing? Like Frank, I do wonder when I'll really feel my life has been turned over to God. Will I hear a voice in the night? See a bolt of lightning?)

Frank is a mess, and he keeps thinking he can get

out of it by being helpless. This is pretty common too. There are times when you're so sick and drunk and scared that all you can think is, "Put me in the hospital and keep me there where it's clean and white and the food comes every day." That's not how the hospital is, of course, but the old, sick-at-home-from-school comforts come creeping back. Sure, I'd like to spend the day apart, under the covers. I'd like to lie down too. Why the hell not? I throw a pillow on the couch and lie down and pull myself in like a cat curling.

I'm almost dreaming and the phone rings. I try to make sense of the ringing in the dream world, but can't quite. My eyes pop open, and I grope on the end table for the phone. It falls on the floor. "Shit!" I yell and pick it up.

"Jack?"

"Yeah Frank."

I'll kill him.

"How can I just keep going, Jack? I mean if I don't feel it right, how can I just keep going?"

I shriek, "You think I fucking care? You think anybody cares, you whining ass? You sad-ass chicken shit. Could you leave me alone for ten minutes? All right? You aren't even a good fucking drunk. Go to hell!"

Oh God.

There's a silence.

"Jesus, Jack, okay. Okay."

He hangs up and the phone is making a noise in my hand like a live thing.

So I sit down because I'm on my feet and half-bent, curled, in some kind of raging-mongoose posture and I know exactly what I've done because I've been here plenty of times before. It always worked before, always did what it was supposed to do, but I'm lost now in a sudden emptiness.

I don't even know whether or not the rages are real. I can't remember the first one. Was it a tactic? If it was, it tapped into something demonic. I've never run into anyone who can handle it except by walking away. It's a fall-back position. It's what I do when anyone gets too close to seeing me.

I'm breathing hard and my face is red, so I go to the kitchen and splash water on it.

What can I say to Frank? I could say, "Frank, I'm under enormous pressure, don't want to talk about it now, but things are very tough. I just blew it. I'm sorry." But that wouldn't be quite true, would it?

(The internal dialogue is endless. It's the Twelve Steps moving and shifting and working me at their will. I'm not working the Steps; the Steps are working me. That isn't true. What is true? The Steps are alive but they let me work them.)

"Frank," I say, "I'm really sorry I did that to you. I'm really sorry."

"Sure, Jack."

"It's old stuff, you know; it's how I got when I was drinking, how I got . . . uh . . . how I kept people from finding me out. You know?"

"Sure, Jack."

He doesn't know. "It's an old reflex. It's what I did not to be seen and keep doing whatever I wanted to do."

"Uh-huh."

"I'm sorry."

"It's okay."

"Look, Frank, what I said isn't how I feel. All I really felt was that you were going around in circles and taking me with you. I just snapped."

"Sure."

"Okay, you know what you're doing? You know how every damn thing you hear you have to try to make it airtight before you move an inch off the dime?"

Silence.

"Well you do, Frank. It's like we all try to stay where we are no matter how bad it is. The alcohol says 'stay here,' okay? And it uses what it finds in your head. The mechanism is, it works to keep you where you are. Yours happens to be 'I can think this out of existence; then things will be unclear, and I won't have to do anything.'"

"You think so?"

And the flash of inspiration. "And if you bug the

people who care with endless wheels of what you're thinking, pretty soon they'll turn on you, and then you can really do whatever the hell you want."

"Oh. Oh, okay."

"Pray a little, Frank. Turn your head off."

"Okay."

"And I'm sorry, jeez. I didn't mean that stuff."

When I hang up, I feel like maybe I've helped. Pretty good, I did pretty good. It's already dark.

The Four Feathers is on the tube and I love it, so I get the dishes done, tidy up, read the paper I'd missed in the morning, get all the stuff I'll need, arrange it around me, pretzels too, and settle into the big armchair for two hours with my black-and-white childhood and the world I used to like to think I was born to of high adventure and final redemption.

It's just as good as I remember and about halfway through (Ralph Richardson in the desert, the sun on the back of his neck, the swoon) the front door opens behind me and it's Suzie. She comes in. I know her footsteps, and she stands behind me, watching, and I say, "Hi," not looking up. She takes her coat off, behind me, and throws it on the couch and goes around and perches on it. Out of the corner of my eye, I can see she's wearing the blue dress, and I take a pretzel, eat it, and hand her the bowl without turning. She says, "No, thanks," and we sit there like that for a few minutes. Finally she says, "I didn't know I was coming here to watch television." I fade in a red haze, can feel someone detonating my insides, and that quickly I'm out of control. "Who asked you over?" I screamed. "Who asked you over?"

Oh God, oh God. I can't stop but it's different because I can hear myself and notice that I have tears in my eyes from watching the movie, so I snap my head away from her.

"Are you my whole life now? Do you tell me what to do now? That's not how it is; so get it straight or get out."

I stop. She's gotten slowly off the couch and she's standing there looking at me in perfect fright, tears in her eyes, absolutely terrified. I can feel the tensioned curve in my back and my neck. Something drains away and I try to straighten up.

We haven't said a word.

I straighten.

"Oh God, Suzie, I'm so sorry. I'm so sorry."

"My God, Jack."

"I know. I'm sorry. I'm just wrong, you know? I'm so goddamn wrong and there are things I can't deal with yet and I'm just wrong. Please forgive me. Please. It wasn't me."

"My God. I hope not."

"I get comfortable and I'm hiding and then something breaks in and I get scared and that's what comes out. I get scared that things are expected or something.

I have to live up to something and I get scared and the rage starts up. I'm so sorry."

She could come over to me, and I can see her thinking about it, but she's still scared.

"You didn't sound scared."

"That's what it's supposed to do, cover that part."

"Should I go home?"

I don't know quite what to do, so I turn off the television.

"Well, that's a relief," she says.

This is hell, I think. *I don't want to turn off the television.*

There's one thing in my head that's pretty good. Now I'm entirely ready to have God remove these defects of character.

"I was wrong," I say. *I'm wrong,* I think.

They keep telling me, "Some are sicker than others" and simple as that sounds, it's suddenly a profound insight to me.

I feel free, as if everything simple were mine and I were everything simple.

Chapter
Eleven

Sought through prayer and meditation to improve
our conscious contact with God *as we understood Him,*
praying only for knowledge of His will for us and
the power to carry that out.

*The assumption here is that I already have a conscious contact
with God. My oldest conscious contact with God was an
attempt—praying to a kid's plaster Jesus in the attic moonlight.
My latest is nothing at all.*

*I look at myself as carefully as I can, but all I see or hear in
there is Jack and the murmuring, demented drunk who wants
his fix.*

*But when I look at the Steps, too, and see them flickering, I
know I've come from there to here because I'm not drinking
and because, when things are good and time is behaving itself
and I feel neither larger nor smaller than I am, there's an edge
of a peace quite different from anything I've ever known. Just
an edge, but it's enough when you're not drinking because*

that, by itself, is a miracle since you knew, and you know, that you can't stop.

I look at myself as carefully as I can in a way that's quite apart from the inventory taking, the endless recrimination, or the stupid apprehension.

Because this is where it all is, for me, and I've been lying in the dark for most of my life waiting for someone to talk to me, tell me what to do, how to stop hurting, how not to be afraid, how not to feel myself hanging around my neck like a great dead bird.

Conscious contact with God is the end of the Steps and the process unrolls from there in terms of letting it grow and making myself more capable of doing what I should be doing, what I'm expected to do, which I should be able to feel. Maybe I'll take care of things. Maybe I'll look in my son's eyes and feel nothing but love.

I'm not a complete fool and I know that what I'm dealing with is a very high spiritual discipline. And the great part is that it doesn't have to be seen that way. There's no priesthood to call attention to grades of understanding, no hierarchical language, and it comes by itself when you give up, making no moral judgments or prohibitions, because if you work the Steps, it will no longer be possible for you to drink or maim yourself or anyone else.

And the Steps came from out of nowhere, from a bunch of drunks in a church basement somewhere in the Midwest, drinking coffee, talking it over.

There is no priest who can tell me a damn thing; my expe-

rience of the Church has left a deep anger behind, and it's not going to go away. But there is no priest here, and the only ritual is the holding of hands in a place where everyone knows how empty the solitary mind really is—the flimsy, self-justifying personality.

This is the way I start to think when I step into the Steps. I barely notice. Because the grace is everywhere and because, unlike the kid in the attic with the plaster crucifix in the moonlight, I'm not alone.

I'm holding hands with other human beings who are in pain and looking for a way out that doesn't involve doing any more violence to themselves or anyone else. Or setting themselves above and apart, or grasping at power, or pretending to have knowledge beyond what works.

I have a conscious contact with God in that I'm not a stranger anymore, and I'm healing, and it has nothing to do with my will. It has to do with the grace in the rooms and the unpretentious words. It has to do with the light of the souls in aggregate.

~ ~ ~

I STILL HAVE TO do my laundry and I hate it. The dishes I don't mind so much because I can put my hands in the water, let it run over them, and it's a good thing. It's in the nature of water to tell me to calm down.

Now, I wake up in the morning feeling like a reasonably decent human being; then I let the chaos in, pick out the problem for the day, and pray for help. Then I get up and go about the real stuff, the dishes from the night before, the phone calls about work, the brooding over coffee. I am, for example, the neediest son-of-a-bitch who ever lived and if I don't get something back from Steve soon, I'm going to fall into a serious resentment. What do I want? I want him to tell me he loves me.

Why should he do that, after what I've put him through? Maybe he does, and maybe he doesn't. But why should he want to tell me? To get me off the hook? How many years did I have *him* on the hook? And he was just a little boy with a huge, demented little boy for a father. What was it like?

(I know what it was like—I had one of my own.)

But Christ, can't he just say, "I love you." I'd feel so much better. What could be more important than that? He already said it was over, that he didn't have the rage anymore, so what's the problem?

The problem is I am one sad-ass, unlovable drunk—that's the problem.

(Thirteen years it will take for Steve to say "I love you"—not long at all, really.)

And Christmas is coming, again. It'll never be over. At Christmas they run meetings twenty-four hours a day at the Alano Club, because Christmas really hurts. It's in the nature of the holiday. Everything will be wonderful Christmas morning unless Dad didn't have any money to buy anything or Mom fell into the tree, drunk; unless Dad didn't come home with the stuff in the car or Mom wasn't talking to anyone.

It feels like every bright hope the drunk ever had is hanging on the Christmas tree, by the neck. Then there's the loneliness.

Men and women come to the Alano Club because the whole of the outside world is screaming "Get drunk; after all, it's the holidays!"

My mother is coming again, for Christmas.

(I haven't said anything about making amends to my mother. I just had to go back and look, because I didn't think I could have left her out but sure enough, sure enough.)

Here's how it was.

"Hi, Mom."

"Oh, Jack, I was just thinking about you."

"How are you, Mom?"

"Oh, I'm fine. I'm just sitting down with a little drink before dinner. It relaxes me. I never knew that, but I guess it was all the bad examples around me."

"Be careful. How many do you have?"

"Oh, it's nothing at all, Jack, nothing."

"I need to make amends, Mom. I need to let you know how wrong I was and how sorry I am. About everything, you know."

"Oh, you don't have to say a word to me. Not at all. So long as it's over. You've been so sure before, you know, and I always believe you and then . . ."

"This is a longer time, Mom. This is for real. I haven't had a drink in a year."

"Well, that's fine, Jack, but I just hope you'll be careful. All the friends you always had were drinking too."

"Well, I'm sorry, Mom. I'm an alcoholic. I couldn't stop then and I hate everything I did, but I can't change anything in the past except to tell you how sorry I am."

"Oh, it was awful, you know. I'd cry for a week and then there'd be another call and God knows where from, so I couldn't do anything. I couldn't help and there you were out there going to kill yourself, you said, and what could I do? You're my son out there, God knows where, and you're going to kill yourself and all I've got is the phone. It was so terrible, Jack. I can't even tell you. It was so terrible."

"I know, Mom. I was crazy."

"You can't do it ever again. I couldn't stand it. Then the calls from Pat because you'd always call her too, and what could she do? A married woman with her own life? There wasn't a thing."

"You don't think it out, Mom. I didn't think it out and think, 'Now I'll scare everyone.' It's just what you do. It's the alcohol and the misery."

"I know it was difficult for you growing up, with

your father and all, but it was difficult for all of us, Jack, wasn't it?"

"Yeah, Mom."

"We all had our grief and George did the best he could but he wasn't well; you know that."

"He was a drunk and then they got him addicted to pills, Mom."

"Oh, I guess you're right. We were happy sometimes, weren't we?"

She's getting a little drunk—I can hear the movement into speculative memory, the teary edge to the voice.

"Sure, Mom. I just needed to tell you it wasn't your fault, any of it. I was just being drunk and that's how it is. There wasn't anything you could have done about it because the alcohol's in the family and I just happened to be the one that got it."

"That's the truth, I guess. Your father's family, you know, had a lot of trouble with drinking."

"Well, I'm sorry, Mom."

"It was so terrible, Jack. Is it over for good do you think?"

"It's over."

"Because I couldn't stand it. You have no idea how terrible . . ."

And I'm getting angry, which is terrible, just terrible, because I don't have a leg to stand on and no *right* to get angry, but I am. All the old emotions are coming back. Why didn't she ever protect me from him? I can't stand the feeling. I never *could* stand the emotions, and now I'm trying to make things better and she's throwing me back into Christmas past and that way is pure hell with my nerves like glass.

"I love you, Mom. I have to go now."

"It's wonderful, Jack, what you're doing. I'll see you soon. It will be wonderful to see the children again. How is Sarah?"

"She's fine, Mom. Have to run."

"Okay, Jack. You were a sunny little boy, early on. Do you remember that?"

"Not really. Bye, Mom."

"What will you be doing for Thanksgiving?"

"I guess we'll have dinner."

"Well, I'll be out on the twenty-first for Christmas. If it's all right, I mean."

"Of course it's all right. The kids will be here."

"You're not in the terrible little apartment anymore?"

"No, Mom."

"Well, that's good. I just knew you'd drink again in there."

"Yeah, Mom."

I put the phone down and pretend to think. I do a lot of that. I sit and look at my hands, the carpet, and act like I'm thinking. What's in my head though is just a stew of emotions and pictures. It's okay. They sort out after a while.

Chapter Eleven

It's three days before my AA birthday.

I'm going to go to a chip meeting and get a colored plastic chip that says "1 Year" on it. I already have the 1 Day, 30 Days, and 6 Months chips. They're a nice, smooth plastic. I don't carry them around but if I did, they'd be nice to feel in my pocket—smooth and substantial.

It's been a year and I haven't been drunk. I started drinking when I was eight, with the wine in the sacristy, but I didn't really kick off as a drunk till I was a teenager.

(No. I was a drunk when I was eight with red wine spread out through every cell in my body like God himself, like the promise of eternal exhilaration and perfect fearlessness.)

I was drunk for most of my life, so I have to learn everything all over again because what you learn when you're drinking doesn't stick, and when you go back to it, you feel like a novice, an impostor.

Which is how I always felt. A lot of emotions seem to be the same, but I wonder how they look from the outside—how my emotions are perceived, how the actions that come off them are judged?

(If nothing else, I've learned that others who know what's going on are usually better able to tell me how I'm doing than I am. This is a very deep and important recognition. It draws me into community, astonished, and leaves me open to the world.)

If I went by my past, thought the way I always did, I'd be drunk pretty quick. If I went back to being who I was right before I got drunk, I'd be drunk pretty quick. If I kept my emotions at bay, doing what I'd always done, I'd be drunk pretty quick. Odds are I'll be drunk pretty quick.

Except. Except.

Something is different. I'm *inside* something and inside the controlling emotion is peace and I can always go there, always. Sometimes it takes a while, and sometimes TK has to knock me on the head, but I can get inside where the emotions are peace and certainty.

The peace comes from the glow in the rooms, when things are suddenly right, and the certainty comes from the split second when I wake up and there I am. I'm not sick and I'm not drunk, and what I did the day before can be looked at without the shudder, horror, and the "I can't make it any different" endlessness.

I'm inside the Steps and the Steps leave me open and vulnerable. So what Step am I on? I'm improving my conscious contact with God. Do I have a conscious contact with God? I'm conscious of God; the contact isn't willable. I feel like I'm doing the right things, because I'm conscious. If I want to take the Eleventh Step, I have to make conscious contact with God.

(Slow down and breathe.)

How do I do that? I take the First Step.

(In giving up is all my strength, so I give up.)

Chapter Eleven

When the convolutions set in and the committee is meeting in my head and there are no simple things left, no joy anywhere, I put my head down and take the First Step. And the Third Step, the Seventh Step, and sometimes when it's bad, I go back again to the Sixth, which is tough, and the Second, which is sanity itself.

And always there's the Twelfth, which I'm up to my eyes in already and have been for a while, because as soon as you find yourself inside the Steps, inside a roomful of people gathered together in the name of humanity, in God's name, you've begun to carry the message. It's simple enough because it's Step One, clear as glass.

There's a Tuesday night chip meeting in a cavernous community center in San Rafael, and that's where I'll get my chip.

I feel like I'm being confirmed without the trappings, the shiny black shoes, and starched white shirt. There's no priest to get in the way.

There must be six or seven hundred people in gray metal folding chairs, and each of them is an equal piece of the room. Looking around, I understand how deeply this community is my community. I know a lot of people. They know me. Some of them have been watching me since I made my first shaky steps, way back when making a commitment to speak would send me straight back to the bottle.

Some of them knew me when I was still Jack the

Lump, with the terrible grapefruit swelling on my forehead. Some of them know me from the bars. Anyone who does know me knows that the odds on me were as bad as they get and that for all practical purposes, I was dead when I came in the door.

TK sits with me and the speaker speaks. She's pretty good—lucid and sad and alive—but I barely hear her because I'm going to get up and go to the front of the room. They'll give me a plastic chip that says "1 Year" on it.

It's my Nobel Prize. It's my visible sign of grace. It's the first thing in years I can take pride in, and the pride is the real stuff, the kind I've barely known at all.

When the speaker is finished, they bring out the chips. The first chip is for anyone with twenty-four hours. Two young guys, a guy in his thirties, and a woman in her fifties get up and start down the aisle. The thirty-year-old is shaking like a leaf. The woman is a little embarrassed, like maybe she's been seen doing it before.

The two younger guys know each other, and they're trying to strut, just a little, but not bringing it off. They take their chips and start back, looking at the chip, looking up, people who know them standing up to touch their shoulders and give encouragement.

"One week," the voice says, and up through the demarcations to, "One year."

I can't remember how my legs are supposed to work.

Chapter Eleven

I'm *terribly* self-conscious (for a salesman, it's practically a psychotic break).

There are three of us—one guy I don't know, a shy woman named Alice, and me. The crowd is applauding wildly, genuinely happy that we made it.

The guys in the crowd who have twenty years aren't patronizing, and the guys with twenty-four hours are looking around surprised because they can feel the utter absence of irony and judgment. The fact is that anyone in the crowd may be feeling anything at all, may be sunk in the most terrible isolation, but when the crowd applauds, everyone is picked up and briefly carried.

There are no requirements here, no power structure, and no dogma beyond "what you give away comes back."

The woman gives me a hug and a chip (human arms around me). On the way back, I have the chip in my hand and it's slippery from sweat. Faces pop up in front of me and arms hold me briefly. I'm absolutely transported.

I did it.

After the meeting, I'm sitting with TK and a couple of others in one of those plastic and Naugahyde-booth roadside places, drinking coffee, and TK says, "How does it feel?" and I say, "It feels all right," and I don't think I've ever said that before and meant it.

I'm a pretty decent guy and I'm going to get better.

So it's in a new world and there's room in it for everything I ever was, or felt, or did. And everything I can be too. The only thing there's no room for is the alcohol. I've been lifted up out of nothing, out of fear, and the agent of the lifting was a handful of rooms with free coffee and open understanding.

I've made it through a year; I can make it through anything.

Walking through the coffee shop parking lot, I can feel the night sky all around me, breathable.

I'll still worry about the Steps and turn the Sixth around in my head like an alien object, like a piece of a meteorite. But it doesn't matter whether I'm sure of it or not. "I am powerless over alcohol," I can say, and all the strength in the world flows from the words.

Last year was last year and I remember it perfectly, and somewhere I'll always be squeezing myself through the basement window and backing into the terrible little apartment. Rest in peace.

The Eleventh Step is the simplest of all, next to the Twelfth. Because when I look at it closely, read it for meaning, I find out that all it does is describe my life as I'm living it.

Oh, I think, all the hours of doubt, recrimination, fear, exhaustion, and occasional lovely certainty resolve themselves into "Sought through prayer and meditation . . ."

Oh, I think, *so pass it on.*

Chapter Eleven

Mom shows up on the twenty-first and I drive down to the airport to get her. I don't bring the kids along because I have an idea in my head that maybe we can talk now, maybe say some heartfelt things. I'm a little late, and she's off the plane already, looking around brightly, the very epitome of a good Irish-Catholic mother with coiffed white hair and birdlike attention.

"Oh, there you are, Jack. Thank goodness. I got so worried for a bit."

"You don't have to worry. I'm okay."

"Well, that's certainly wonderful. All those times we had such high hopes, you know."

(Jesus, Mom, shut up.)

I pick up her bags at the carousel and off we go. It's a chilly, bright day. I don't have the van anymore and I'm really happy about that.

"How's everybody?"

"You mean Pat, dear? And Karl?"

"Yeah. Everybody."

"As well as can be expected. They all send their best."

"Karl sends his best?"

"Maybe not Karl," she says, and laughs, which is nice, that she can laugh at the grudges I've earned.

"Think he'll come around?"

"Oh, he might, but we've all seen it so many times before, you know."

(Shut up, Mom.)

"Your father would be proud, Jack. Real proud."

(A sinking feeling. A sad, cold presence.)

"Yeah, Mom."

"We didn't know then all that they know now about the drink and pills."

"That's true."

The Golden Gate Bridge rises and falls away. I reach in my pocket and take out my chip and hand it to her.

"Oh, isn't that nice. They give these out then?"

"Yeah."

"Well that's very nice and you must be proud."

"I am. I'm very proud."

"I never gave up, Jackie, I never did. When you'd call, I'd always think, God will help him. I'd go to church and I'd tell Pat, too, to pray. I don't know how many prayers I and others prayed for you—thousands and thousands."

"I guess they did the job."

(A little anger, there, a little rage there thinking about some anonymous priest in some goddamn Missouri chapel sticking my name in a prayer and that's what did it, that's the whole game.)

"Oh, I wouldn't say that, Jack. They helped you along, I'm sure, but it was your strength that got you through and we always knew you had it."

(Is Mom subtle? Is she leading me places?)

"I pray a lot."

"You go to Mass? You were always such a devout little boy."

"No, Mom. I just pray."

"Well, I'm sure Our Lord hears you. You were always so serious and devout."

"We used to drink the communion wine. Did you know that? Harry Book and I used to knock it down in the sacristy. We were drunk altar boys."

She laughs, I swear to God.

"I'm sure you weren't the first."

"Remember Dad would cry and make me pray to the Virgin for him?"

"Yes, I do. And you did it very well. We all knew how sick he was, but what are you going to do? We all just tried our best till he died. And maybe he found some peace."

(The conversation is slipping away from me. I had things I wanted to say. What were they?)

"Maybe he found some peace because he had so little here on earth."

(My life is unmanageable.)

"Are you working, Jackie? Have you found a job?"

(Mom is relentless.)

"I had a job but it's over. I'm looking for another one."

"As long as you're careful now, I'm sure anybody would be glad to have you."

(There's an edge of laughter in my head. It feels all right.)

"Maybe you could start in retail sales. Like shoes or something."

(Oh my mother, oh the sweet little thing.)

"Sure, Mom."

"It would only be for a little while, you know."

(Oh human beings and effort and love in the wrong words and endless, helpless flailing with flesh of our flesh.)

She hands me back the chip. It feels terrific in my hand.

"Great to see you, Mom. Great you could come."

As soon as we get back to the house, she wants to go to the store and buy the things she's going to need.

One of the things she'll need is a bottle of vodka.

"I hope you don't mind, Jack. It does relax me before dinner."

"No, Mom, I don't mind."

The kids watch her and watch me. The kids are quite taken with the notion of watching me watch *my* parent get drunk. Should I say something? Should I say, "Mom, you've got a problem"? Does she have a problem? Jesus, it's Christmas with her grandchildren and a son who put on his father's oversize shoes to jump up and down on her life just the way he had.

She's an old lady, and she gets a little silly before dinner. "Remember when . . . ," she says, and the memories are all bright and lively.

I look at her as quietly as I can. She's lovely and bright and charming, and she tells the kids stories I'd rather not hear again, though they've never heard them, and she takes little sips from her drink. Once, she gets up to show them a vaudeville kick and a twirl. She remembers to put her drink down first and, "Well, if nothing else," she says, "you certainly raised some lovely children, Jackie, through it all." The table lamp is reflecting in Steve's glasses so I can't see (never quite can), Bridget is beaming, and Dave is bringing her some kind of stuff on crackers.

We're all there in the room, in the light, and it feels good, like home, which is to say a place where people are at ease with each other. Mom with her tipsy chatter and her twirls has pulled the room together so I can feel what it should have been like all those years.

And I love us all, even me.

Mom's no drunk. She's just a tipsy old lady who's finally come home too.

Chapter Twelve

Having had a spiritual awakening as the result of these steps, we tried to carry this message to alcoholics, and to practice these principles in all our affairs.

~ ~ ~

HELL YES, I can do that.

And so I can. I've been doing it all year. *We've* been doing it all year.

Epilogue

YOU HAVE TO *FEEL* THE ROOMS. There are nights when every word a speaker says is perfect, the breathing is perfect, the attention is perfect, and there's nothing but emotion and the recognition of truth, which makes the emotion bearable.

(There are nights, too, when nothing is right, but nothing bad happens, and we breathe and move on.)

And no one ever says any of what has to be said in precisely the same way because no one is expected to, because there *is* no one set of words sanctified by a central authority. There's only the light generated by drunks helping each other.

I came to the meetings with a mind full of violent misery and looping self-pity—broken, hallucinating, weeping, dead, and buried alive. A *thing*, really, trying to move into life.

Now I can put out my hand and say, "Do you

need some help?" I now know I have some to offer—simpleminded Jackie with his broken heart, shimmering incompetence, and bellyful of communion wine.

I don't feel sorry for myself (except when I drop the toast on the kitchen floor, the morning paper is all wet, or another day goes by without Steve calling up to say, "I love you, Dad"), so I'm able to help the guy across the way.

The Steps move deeper and deeper and get more and more translucent. When they stop (they don't, really), it's right at the heart of the answer. I am not alone or afraid because I help others and they help me and the medium of the help doesn't diminish, but passes from hand to hand.

I can't imagine a more perfect passage than the move into sobriety, because it has no limiting factors, no definitions beyond Now—a place where we are all safe, sober, and sane, for the most part.

In groups, I never hear, "This is good and that evil"; or "We are good and they are not"; or "These are the words *we* say that *they* don't know and we need to protect them"; or "I know and you don't because I am worthy and you are not." Never. There's nothing but the flickering light that comes and goes with the sense that we're doing the best we can, for the first time, and that our power doesn't look for more power but relaxes back into love and roams around the room.

In every meeting some are sicker than others; in

every room there are some who won't make it and will die alone, sodden, and terrified. Everybody knows it. No one is ever turned away. Guys go out and get drunk, and when they come back, all they hear is, "Welcome back." You introduce yourself as a newcomer and get on with it.

There are no rules beyond the offering of the truth, and when you've gone as far as you can go trying to help someone, you can turn him over to God, to himself, and hope it works out.

There was a guy who slept on my couch and complained about my coffee. He littered every room with his bankruptcy papers, gave himself airs, blustered and huffed about the Big Book (which he had memorized and used to keep people off his case), and generally marked time in the program until he was ready to go out and get drunk again, which he'd do, then come back contrite and full of new understanding of some paragraph in the book, how *it* had been the problem, how he hadn't really got the One Big Little Thing. Now he was ready, and would I mind . . .

Finally there's that moment, and you know you've gone as far as you can go—and two steps farther—and you say "no more."

His lady friend called me up one morning and said, "Jack, Teddy's really sick. He's been out again and he's really bad. You're the only one he can think of to call. He asked me to call."

"Fine, tell you what Nancy, in about ten minutes have him downstairs in front of the house, in the street, and I'll drive by and run him over."

She laughed.

Teddy didn't die. He just moved on to someone else and I don't know to this day how it turned out, but I know that there would always be a room open to him and that whatever effort he was willing to put out, he'd get back, doubled. If he didn't give up, he probably died alone, scared, and all there is for anyone to say is "Rest in peace" or "There but for the grace of God go I."

"We claim spiritual progress rather then spiritual perfection," it says in the book.

I've never really heard anyone claim even that. Nobody comes to a meeting and says, "Hey, I made a bunch of spiritual progress last week and I know some stuff that you don't."

No spiritual one-upmanship, no rising above the pain of others in pursuit of the Higher Calm. But we do make spiritual progress, and because there's *real* community, the individual can go his own way.

I'm no paragon. I don't know anyone in the program who is. We were weak, sick, terrified drunks and we joined together to get out of our own heads.

We weren't *really* weak of course; the strength it takes to lead an alcoholic life could lift an aircraft carrier. All that strength—yes, even willpower—does is maintain the structure, the dim scaffolding we use to keep ourselves moving from one drink to the next. The strength all goes into self-will run riot and the support of six thousand pounds of barely movable iron piping on casters.

The Steps don't weigh anything, and when the fear comes, they light up—now here, now there. Like the eyes you see in the room, the human eyes with human light in the great other-light; picking it up, shining, flickering, and almost touchable. There's a being and a process here and neither diminishes because neither ever becomes property.

Something comes in to your hands and they're different. Something gets passed along and you're different.

This is less a body of knowledge (though it is that, and rigorously empirical) and more a body of light in which the broken and the powerless come together slowly in the understanding that power is nothing at all, and powerlessness is a gift and from it comes all strength.

You just put out your hand, and there's something in it.

So this book, if it hasn't helped, at least it's done no harm. If it has helped, it's done what it wanted to do and we both have more than we started with.

In the light, the rooms full of drunks are an idea of heaven—the eyes fixed on the good, stirring and circling like the breath of God.

About the Authors

JACK ERDMANN

An accomplished salesman and businessman, Jack Erdmann is also an author and lecturer in the San Francisco area. A fourth-generation alcoholic, he has been sober for more than twenty years.

LARRY KEARNEY

Larry Kearney was born in Brooklyn in 1943, moved to San Francisco in 1964, and has since published eleven books of poetry. He had his last drink in 1981.